Brassey's *History of Uniforms*

Brassey's *History of Uniforms*

American Civil War Confederate Army

By Ron Field

Colour plates by Richard Hook

Series editor Tim Newark

To Jane, Daniel, and Jaime

First English Edition 1996

UK editorial offices: Brassey's Ltd, 33 John Street, London
WC1N 2AT
UK Orders: Marston Book Services, PO Box 269, Abingdon,
Oxford OX14 4SD

North American Orders: Brassey's Inc,
PO Box 960, Herndon, VA 22070, USA

Ron Field has asserted his moral right to be identified as the
author of this work.

Library of Congress Cataloging in Publication Data available
British Library Cataloguing in Publication Data
A catalogue record for this book is available from the British
Library

ISBN 1 85753 162 0 Hardcover

Typeset and printed in Great Britain by Images Book
Production Ltd.

Contents

Introduction

The image of the 'ragged rebel' of the Confederate Army has long stalked the pages of American Civil War history. A tattered grey jacket, nondescript trousers, and shapeless slouch hat have all too often been accepted as the archetypal Southerner. This study, which is the result of nearly twenty years of research, sets out to create a fuller understanding of what the Confederate soldier really wore - from the first heady days of secession in South Carolina in 1860, to the fall of Richmond, Virginia, in 1865. It also attempts to explain reasons for the rise and fall in the availability of uniforms as the war progressed.

In each of the eleven states which joined the Confederacy during 1861 (plus the three 'border states') floods of volunteers to the Southern cause donned pre-war militia dress, or had new service uniforms made up by local tailors, or by their own womenfolk. The variety, cut, and colour of these early war uniforms was endless. Inevitably, confusion reigned on the battlefields of Big Bethel and First Manassas, as friend mistook foe - often with fatal consequences. With the approach of the first winter of war, and the realisation that the Confederate Government was ill-prepared to clothe those troops entering its service, the first 'Great Appeal' for clothing was issued throughout the Southern press. With the help of countless 'volunteer aid societies', composed mainly of the wives, daughters, and sweethearts of those at the battlefront, many soldiers received a new suit of mainly grey clothes, an overcoat, a blanket, a pair of socks. Thus they survived the rigours of the first winter of war.

The winter of 1861-62 also saw the beginning of some central issuance of uniforms by the Confederate Quartermaster Department established at Richmond, Virginia. But too little was made available too slowly, and many men were reduced to unnecessary suffering in rags and barefeet. Hence each state began to produce its own, often quite distinctive, pattern of uniform, generally funded by the Confederate commutation system begun in July 1861, which provided that each enlisted man should receive $21 (later $25) every six months for clothing.

As the war progressed through the years, so did the uniform appearance of the Confederate soldier, at least in the eastern theatre of the conflict. But what the North Carolina 'Tarheel' wore differed greatly from that of his counterpart from Georgia or Mississippi. Although grey, based mainly on C.S. Army Regulations of 1861, became the colour of cloth common to all, many different shades and hues were created out of shortage and neccessity.

The summer of 1862 came and went. It was disaster in the West, and victory in the East. General Braxton Bragg's Perryville/Kentucky campaign was disappointing, while Lee held his ground at Antietam, and Fredericksburg. By the Fall of 1862, both Armies were again poorly clad. The C.S. Quartermaster Department was embarrassed and assailed. Soldiers were writing home for clothes, and a second 'Great Appeal' was issued from Richmond for warm winter clothing. The States again responded, but this time North Carolina and Georgia shut out the speculators and Quartermaster agents, and declared that they would clothe their own men first, and the Confederate government could have what was left!

By early 1863, Quartermaster Department clothing workshops had been established in Columbus and Augusta, as well as Richmond, to make uniforms for the exclusive use of its own Bureaus. Those states that wished to clothe their own first were left alone for the present. By 1863 an increasing amount of imported clothing was coming through the blockade, while further manufacturing centres had been set up. By the Fall of 1863, Confederate soldiers in some battles and campaigns were described as being better dressed than those in the Federal army.

By early 1864, both the Army of Tennessee, and the Army of Northern Virginia, were in plentiful receipt of Quartermaster Depot uniforms of a similar

pattern, if not the same kind of cloth. At the end of that year, with Atlanta and Vicksburg taken, and most of Tennessee in Northern hands, it was back to rags and barefeet for many Confederate soldiers. The Army of Tennessee, destroyed at Franklin and Nashville, were reduced to wearing captured Federal clothing. According to quartermaster reports, those around Petersburg, Virginia, remained well clothed. Elsewhere, the dissolving armies wandered about the country while the factories continued to produce and the storehouses held supplies that could not be moved to the troops. By April 1865 it was all over, although at the surrender of Confederate forces under General Joseph E. Johnston at Durham Station on 26th of that month, North Carolina alone had on hand 92,000 sets of uniforms, and vast stores of blankets and leather.

The Charleston Zouave Cadets were formed on 17 August 1860 and modelled themselves on Elmer E. Ellsworth's United States Zouave Cadets. This group study was taken during the winter of 1860/61, when secession fever was at its height in South Carolina. First Lieutenant Charles Edward Gilchrist, who commanded the unit at this time, is seated second from the right. Third Lieutenant Benjamin M. Walpole is sat next to him, third from right. The enlisted men wear their 'winter uniform' consisting of chasseur tunic and trousers, and are holding Model 1841 'Mississippi' rifles with brass furniture and patch boxes. Note the 'Tiger head' on the two-piece brass belt plates worn by the two men on the left. Valentine Museum.

South Carolina

Following the act of secession on 20 December 1860, the small Republic of South Carolina began to organise an army of defence in preparation for an inevitable Northern invasion. The militia of the 'Palmetto State' by that time consisted of five divisions, each composed of two brigades of either five or six regiments of generally non-uniformed beat militia, or heavy infantry. Attached to most of these regiments were several companies of uniformed volunteer militia consisting of either light infantry or riflemen. A regiment of uniformed volunteer militia cavalry was also attached to each brigade. The 17th Regiment of Infantry, the 1st Regiment of Rifles, and 1st Regiment of Artillery, of the 4th Brigade, 2nd Division, at Charleston were exceptions to this rule being composed entirely of uniformed companies. Small volunteer battalions at Columbia and Beaufort were also uniformed.

Professor Charles A.H. Peck conducted a military academy in Camden, South Carolina, at the outbreak of the Civil War. Youths like these, in their shell jackets and military caps, went on to the Arsenal and Citadel military academies, and provided a future officer corps for the 'Palmetto State'. Professor Peck, who died of illness on 19 June 1863, is probably stood in the back row wearing a top hat. Camden Archives.

Henry Middleton Rutledge was photographed at the studio of Quinby & Company in Charleston wearing the uniform of the Rutledge Mounted Riflemen, a volunteer militia unit organised on 9 November 1860. His grey coatee was bordered with one-inch wide orange braid, and his grey pants were made 'small at the ankle and fastened by a strap of tape', and had orange worsted seam stripes. A 'French fatigue cap, of blue cloth, with the letters R.M.R. upon the front', as prescribed for this unit, is held in his left hand. North Carolina Division of Archives and History.

As early as October 1860, many of the Charleston companies were beginning to think about the adoption of fatigue clothing or 'service uniforms'. Towards this end they were prompted by several of the military outfitters and hatters of the city. Steele & Co., 'Military Hatters' on King Street, advertised a large stock of 'Fatigue Caps' priced between '50 cents, $1 or $1.25,' adding 'There is no use of being killed in a Ten Dollar Hat'! During January 1861, Walter Steele advertised 'Blue and Gray Cloth Fatigue Caps', 'Glazed Fatigue Caps', and 'Black and Brown Felt Hats, suitable for Military Companies'. Merchant tailor and draper H. Koppel, also on King Street, had supplied 'cheap, excellent and serviceable' fatigue uniforms to units including the Charleston Riflemen, the Palmetto Guard, the Meagher Guard, and the Washington Light Infantry. C.F. Jackson & Company made up uniforms for companies such as the Moultrie Guards, the Vigilant Rifles, the Cadet Riflemen, and the Ætna Guards.

Most of these uniforms were made of some shade of grey cloth, but there the similarity ended. On 21 April 1861, William H. Russell, correspondent for *The Times* of London, wrote:

'At the present moment, Charleston is like a place in the neighbourhood of a military camp where military and volunteer tailors are at work trying experiments in uniforms, and sending their animated models for inspection. There is an endless variety - often of ugliness - in dress and equipment and nomenclature among these companies. The head-dress is generally, however, a smart cap like the French kepi; the tunic is of different cuts, colors, facings, and materials - green with gray and yellow, gray with orange and black and white, blue with white and yellow facings, roan, brown, burnt sienna and olive - jackets, frocks, tunics, blouses, cloth, linen, tweed, flannel.'

The uniformed companies of the Charleston regiments were the first South Carolinians to see active service. The 1st Regiment of Rifles, elements of which occupied Castle Pinckney in Charleston Harbor

An officer in the dark blue 'Volunteer Forces' uniform prescribed for those who received commissions in the regiments raised by the 'Palmetto State' at the beginning of 1861. Buttons were white metal and trousers stripes were white. From a photograph by Ron Field.

which laced up as high as the calf of the leg, and fitted 'snugly over the feet'. The Moultrie Guards wore a 'blue cloth cap, a gray jacket … made of North Carolina (cassimere) goods, with standing collar, and one row of palmetto buttons in front, and black pants'. The Carolina Light Infantry adopted 'Black Pants and Fatigue Jacket.'

The Charleston Zouave Cadets first saw service in 'a neat undress grey suit, with white cross belts.' They also adopted a 'full dress Zouave uniform,' subsequently referred to as a 'winter uniform', which consisted of a grey, nine button chasseur jacket with four- to five-inch skirt, slit in the sides. Modelled on the *habit-tunique* adopted by the French Army in 1860, the jacket worn by the Zouave Cadets had a solid red collar, narrow red braid on the front and bottom edges, red shoulder straps secured by single small buttons, and slash (a tailoring term for an opening on the outside of a cuff closed by two or more buttons) pointed red cuffs fastened with two small buttons. It was apparently without the belt loops often found on chasseur jackets. Most of the jackets worn by the Charleston unit had external pockets on the breast. Non-commissioned officers' chevrons were worn above the elbow with points up.

Trousers were also grey with red seam stripes, and cut in the chasseur style, probably being gathered at the waist with pleats, and below the knee into wide cuffs fastened by buckles or buttons. These were worn with white buttoned gaiters, over which were russet leather *jambiere*, or greaves, buckled at the top and laced down the side opening. Red cadet-pattern caps with lighter-coloured bands, of the small-crowned chasseur pattern were worn with this uniform. Black oilskin covers were required for winter wear.

The uniform worn by officers of the Charleston Zouave Cadets at the time the 'winter uniform' was adopted consisted of a dark blue, nine-button frock coat with red collar and cuffs edged with gold braid, the cuffs being slash and pointed, the back seam being fastened by three small buttons. Rank was indicated by Federal-style shoulder straps with red ground, and a crimson net waist sash. Straight-legged dark blue trousers were trimmed with broad gold-coloured seam stripes. Their red caps resembled those of other ranks but were embellished with one or more horizontal stripes of quarter-inch gold braid encircling the band; above them similar stripes rose vertically to a circle of braid around the top of the crown. The Austrian knot usually associated with this pattern appears not to have been adopted by the Zouave Cadet officers.

Companies of the 17th Regiment, of Charleston, wore an equally diverse range of service uniforms. The

on 27 December 1860, wore a variety of service dress. The Washington Light Infantry had adopted a cadet grey cassimere frock coat, overcoat and pants, the latter being trimmed with three-quarter inch wide black seam stripes; a 'plain felt, brownish color' hat looped up on one side; and 'Leggins of calf-skin,'

Union Light Infantry, a unit with many Scottish members, wore a 'Scotch bonnet, [and] blue hunting shirt and pants'. The 'camp suit' chosen by the Palmetto Guard consisted of a 'grey woollen jacket and pants,' described as being made 'of light grey Kersey trimed [sic] with yellow braid'. Their headgear consisted of 'a blue French Cap'.

Volunteer companies raised by the Charleston Fire Department also adopted a variety of uniforms. The Ætna Guards wore 'a grey pea jacket, trimmed with red, grey pants, and the "kepi" with the initials Æ. G. in gilt letters'. The Phoenix Rifles paraded in frock

William R. Atkinson joined the Richland Volunteer Rifle Company on 1 January 1861, the day it left Columbia for Charleston. He wears the grey pleated hunting shirt of this unit over his civilian clothing. Note the six-pointed star pinned to his neck tie and silver M1834 horn on his fatigue cap. South Caroliniana Library.

coat and pants of 'bluish-Gray plains' trimmed with black braid, and a cap of 'Blue Cloth of recent French military style, with the letters P R [white] in front'. The Vigilant Rifles uniform was made of 'the excellent product of the Rock Island Mills, near Charlotte,

Richland Volunteer Rifle Company, Co. A, 1st South Carolina Volunteers (Gregg's). From a photograph by Ron Field.

North Carolina,' and consisted of a shell jacket and pants of dark grey cassimere trimmed with scarlet braid, and 'a light French fatigue cap of blue, with the initials V. R. in gold embossed'.

Regarding artillery companies of the volunteer militia, the Lafayette Artillery of Charleston acquired an undress uniform by April 1861 which, according to a photograph taken of the unit on Cole's Island by Osborn & Durbec, consisted of a five-button sack coat

or smock, probably light grey in colour, worn loose without waist belt, with two large, waist level patch pockets at the front. The falling collar was trimmed in solid dark-coloured cloth, probably red in line with the unit's dress uniform of blue and red. Cuffs were similarly trimmed with upper edge forming an inverted 'V' shape, whilst the front buttoning edge and top of the pockets were also embellished with a wide band of trim. Trousers were the same colour as the coat, with a narrow dark-coloured stripe on outer seams. Headgear consisted of the Model 1858 forage cap, which was essentially a non-rigid version of the M1851 dress cap with only the top of the crown stiffened. Solid grey in colour, and apparently trimmed with a thin band of dark-coloured cord round the top edge, some of these caps were decorated with a small brass crossed cannon insignia, either side of which were the brass letters 'L' and 'A'.

During November 1860, the 'Zouave Drill Club' of the German Artillery of Charleston had adopted a fatigue suit consisting of 'a grey satinet jacket, bound with yellow braid; French undress cap, with glazed cover; and dark pants'. The Beaufort Volunteer Artillery appeared in 'a French fatigue cap, a blue frock coat with standing collar, and a single row of Palmetto buttons on the breast; pants blue with red stripes' during the same month.

The Charleston Light Dragoons, renowned for their 'Bottle Green' coatee with 'trimmings of red Casimere'; 'Helmet of black Patent leather trimmed with brass' and 'white horse hair' plume, had their 'Measures taken for the Service Uniform' on 28 November, and paraded in 'full Fatigue Dress' on 11 December 1860. A visitor to Charleston during January 1861 described this as consisting of a 'small French military cap' and fatigue jacket: '... charily trimmed with red worsted, and stained with the rains and earth of the islands. One young dragoon in this sober dress walked into our hotel, trailing the clinking steel scabbard of his sabre across the marble floor of the vestibule with a warlike rattle'.

The only state uniform regulations in use at this time were for officers and were modelled on the antiquated U.S. pattern of 1839. Clearly something more modern was needed for the officers of the State Volunteer Forces being grafted on to the existing South Carolina militia system by an act of 17 December 1860. The new regulations subsequently published by the State Adjutant General and entitled *Uniform and Dress of the Officers of the Volunteer Forces*, consisted of a plain dark blue frock coat of M1851 U.S. army pattern, with dark blue trousers and forage caps. General officers wore gilt buttons bearing 'the palmetto device' and gold lace seam stripe on trousers. Silver metal and white leather and facings, abandoned as a distinction for U.S. infantry officers in 1851, were retained as the infantry branch service colour by South Carolina. Hence, field and company grade officers wore silver metal buttons, with white leather sword belts. Field officers' trousers bore one inch-wide silver seam stripes, while those of company grade officers were white. Insignia for the 'dark blue cloth military caps' of company-grade officers consisted of a 'silver palmetto tree on the front, with the figure indicating the number of the Regiment on one side, and the letter R on the other.' Full dress headgear for field officers was the plumed cocked hat prescribed for the state militia in 1839. For undress, they wore forage caps with a silver wreath encircling the figure indicating the number of their respective regiment.

The eight regiments commanded by these officers initially wore a wide variety of uniforms. Whether formed by existing uniformed volunteer militia companies, or raised amongst the ranks of the beat militia, each company was originally provided with a 'service uniform' generally paid for by public subscription, and made up by local tailors and seamstresses. A style of 'hunting shirt' with pleats on the chest and broad band of trim around the skirts was uniquely associated with South Carolina. The Richland Volunteer Rifle Company left Columbia in January 1861 to become Company A of Colonel Maxcy Gregg's 1st South Carolina Volunteers (six months volunteers), wearing a dark grey hunting shirt made from cloth produced at the Rock Island Mills, at Charlotte, North Carolina. Pleats embellished the chest, whilst the trim below the waist was probably green if based on their volunteer militia uniform, which was a 'dark blue green frock coat, trimmed with three rows of gilt buttons ... faced with green velvet'. A forage cap and dark grey trousers completed the service uniform of this company, although they also appear to have worn the U.S. Model 1858 dress hat, or Hardee hat, associated with their militia full dress uniform.

The Rhett Guard of Newberry enlisted as Company L of Colonel Maxcy Gregg's 1st South Carolina in January 1861 wearing 'a fatigue dress, composed of a hunting frock of green, with scarlet sash and oil-silk cap.' During July of the same year this company received new 'outfits for the service' consisting of a grey pleated hunting shirt and pants trimmed with green velvet, and dark coloured slouch hats pinned by star-shaped insignia, with black ostrich feather plumes. The Pee Dee Rifles of Darlington became Company D of Gregg's re-organised 1st South Carolina

Peterson Borrum Ramage enlisted in the Rhett Guard, Co. L, 1st South Carolina Volunteers (Gregg's) on 27 July 1861. Hence his uniform was probably part of the 'outfits for the service' furnished by Mrs. Robert Stewart during that month. S.C. Confederate Relic Room & Museum.

Volunteers, and during the summer of 1861 received a uniform '...of dark grey goods manufactured at Salem, North Carolina. The bodies of the coats were pleated, making a neat appearance and proving, in the absence of overcoats, warm and serviceable.' The Gist Riflemen of Williamston, in Anderson District, were wearing a 'green, hunter-like, loose-fitting coat' when they paraded in front of President Davis within the ranks of the infantry battalion of the Hampton Legion at Camp Chimborazo, near Richmond, on 8 July 1861.

Other South Carolinian companies volunteering for Confederate service wore single-breasted frock coats with the distinctive broad bands of trim around the skirts. The Edisto Rifles of Orangeburg enlisted as Company A of Colonel Johnson Hagood's 1st South Carolina Volunteers (twelve months volunteers) wearing their volunteer militia uniform consisting of a grey frock coat fastened by eight buttons, with a standing collar faced with green, and wide band of green velvet edging on coat skirts. Their grey pants had green seam stripes, and their dark-coloured fatigue caps bore the brass letters 'ER' on the front. On 27 October 1861 the Brooks Grays, Company G of the 7th South Carolina Volunteers (Bacon's), received a new uniform, courtesy of the Ninety-Six Aid Association of Edgefield District. Made of 'gray

John Edward Harrell (or Horrell), of an unidentified South Carolina regiment, wears distinctive South Carolina trim around the skirts of his grey frock coat. The small brass 'Palmetto Tree' which graces the front of his cap dates back to 1840, and was often worn on leather cockades and dragoon helmets. David Wynn Vaughan collection.

cloth', their frock coats were fastened by nine 'silver Palmetto buttons,' and had solid black velvet collars and a narrow band of black velvet trim around the skirts. Their grey trousers had black seam stripes, whilst their grey forage caps had black bands and brass 'Palmetto Tree' insignia in front. The Southern Guards, another company in the 7th South Carolina, were supplied with a uniform of 'dark grey with brilliant orange stripes' on 27 October 1861.

The companies of the infantry battalion of the Hampton Legion originally wore a variety of uniforms off to war in Virginia. That of the Washington Light Infantry Volunteers was described as 'cadet grey, frock coat and pants, with black trimmings; black felt hat, looped up on the left side with a Palmetto cockade.' The green hunting shirt of the Gist Riflemen has already been described. The Davis Guards wore a dark grey or black frock coat and pants with either brown or black felt hats. The South Carolina Zouave

Volunteers, raised initially from the ranks of the Charleston Zouave Cadets, left Charleston to join the Legion wearing 'a grey jacket, well lined, and trimmed with blue. The pants of yellow woollen, very loose about the body, tight around the ankles, so as to go under a gaiter.' Their cap probably consisted of 'a red turban, lined inside with grey, so as to be used either way.' Overcoats were grey, and 'Undershirts' were made of grey flannel.

The Regular Army of South Carolina was established in late December 1860, and consisted of one regiment of infantry, which was eventually designated the 3rd Regiment, South Carolina Artillery; a battalion of artillery, which was expanded and re-organised into the 1st Regiment, South Carolina Artillery; a squadron of cavalry, which later evolved into the Dismounted Dragoon Battalion; and a 'Corps of Military Engineers'. Volunteers enlisted as 'regulars' were informed that their uniform would be 'the same as that of the U.S. Army'. Certainly, officers' dress was based on M1857 U.S. Army regulations, which in general terms consisted of a dark blue frock coat, sky blue trousers, with the kepi, or 'new U.S. Army fatigue cap', replacing the Hardee hat and dress cap.

Regarding the uniform worn by enlisted men of the Regular Army, the 'Clothing Emporium' of C. F. Jackson, 199 King Street, Charleston, was reported in the press to have 'filled numerous orders for ... uniforms for the regular service' by 14 February 1861. A report entitled 'Carolina Caps - Williams & Brown' indicates that this firm was busily engaged 'filling a large order for the South Carolina Army of the regular line'. Artists' impressions of the bombardment of Fort Sumter depict the artillery battalion wearing forage caps and plain uniform trousers. Several wear shell jackets. Company A of this unit was photographed in battle order standing by the guns of Fort Moultrie in caps, plain grey coats and grey pants with dark-coloured seam stripes. During August 1861, several published descriptions of deserters from the Regulars are of value. Private William Bond of Company C, Battalion of Artillery, was described as wearing his 'Uniform Coat, Cap and White Pants' when he went missing from duty at Fort Sumter on 8 August 1861. Private Albert Leildke, of the Third Company (C), 1st Regiment of Infantry, was similarly clad in a 'Uniform Coat, and Cap marked 1, C.S.A., and white pants' when he disappeared from Sullivan's Island the next day!

Several regimental uniforms were also supplied by the State to its volunteer forces. That received by Gregg's original regiment of 1st South Carolina Volunteers (six months state service), consisted of

frock coats and pants of 'dark grey cloth', and was made up under the direction of the Rev. A. Toomer Porter, an Episcopal priest and proprietor of the 'Industrial School for Girls' in Ashley Street, Charleston. In his memoir, *Four Years in Rebel Capitals*, Thomas Cooper DeLeon recalled the 'dirty gray and tarnished silver' of Gregg's regiment arriving in Richmond, which would indicate that they wore white metal state buttons, in line with those prescribed for officers in the Volunteer Forces regulations.

Based on a photograph of Private Joseph Brunson of the Edgefield Riflemen, Company C of Gregg's

Captain W.T. Livingston raised the Keowee Riflemen, later to become Co. A, 1st Regiment of South Carolina Rifles (Orr's Regiments of Rifles), during January 1861. He wears the blue uniform prescribed for this regiment in May 1861. Note the captain's bars on the collar, and two straight strips of braid on his sleeves, representing an oversimplified interpretation of official C.S. regulations. His coat is trimmed, in distinctive South Carolinian style, with a broad band of dark green velvet. His broad, light-coloured trouser stripes do not conform to Orr's Rifles regulations. South Caroliniana Library

Eldred Johnson Kay of the Calhoun Guard, Co. L, Orr's Rifles, died from sickness at Richmond in August, 1862. He wears the enlisted mens' uniform of his regiment, which was blue trimmed with green worsted braid. S.C. Confederate Relic Room & Museum.

unit, the frock coat supplied with this uniform was single-breasted and fastened by nine buttons, and had half-inch wide dark tape trim around the collar, with plain cuffs. His headgear consisted of a grey chasseur pattern forage cap bearing in front the numeral '1' above the letters 'SCV' over 'ER'. Presumably this was one of the caps 'supplied throughout the First South Carolina' by 'Williams and Brown' of King Street in Charleston.

Established in1858 to teach 'plain sewing' to the 'poor girls' of the city, by April 1861 the Rev. Porter had contracted with the Colonel Lewis M. Hatch, of the Quartermaster Department of South Carolina, to supply uniforms for troops in State service. City tailors undertook the 'pressing and cutting' of the cloth, whilst 59 women at his 'Industrial School' worked 32 sewing machines. These labours were variously supplemented by upwards of 350 'out-workers' who presumably sewed by hand. At the end of July 1861, the 'Industrial School' was taken over by the Quartermaster Department. Assisted by Colonel S.L. Glover, Hatch had 'constantly employed ... under the foremanship of Messrs. H. Koppel ["Merchant Tailor" on King Street] and D.H. Kemme ["Draper and Tailor" on Broad Street], forty experienced cutters, who supply about 1500 needlewomen, who make a fair weekly salary.' These two tailors received payment between 14 December 1861 and 31 January 1862 for cutting '3019 frock coats, 1157 overcoats, [and] 113 pair of pants ...'

As chaplain of the Washington Light Infantry Volunteers of Charleston, the Rev. Porter next turned his attention to supplying the Hampton Legion with uniforms to replace those worn off to war which, by August 1861, were 'in rags'. After contacting every factory in Virginia and North Carolina 'in vain for a sufficient quantity of cloth of the same color to uniform one thousand men...', Porter returned to Charleston where he purchased from 'Messrs Wm. Ravenel and Co. ... ten different kinds of cloth for the ten companies' of the Legion. This was duly taken to the State Quartermaster's Department situated at his old 'Industrial School' and turned into frock coats and pants which, by the Fall of 1861, had been delivered to the Hampton Legion.

Evidence for the style of uniform supplied to the Hampton Legion by the Industrial School survives in the frock coat and trousers of Corporal Robert Hayne Bomar, held today by the South Carolina Confederate Relic Room and Museum at Columbia, South Carolina. Bomar enrolled as a private in the Washington Light Infantry Volunteers, Company A of the infantry battalion of the Hampton Legion, on 12 June 1861, and was wounded at First Manassas. Private C.W. Hutson of Bomar's company noted on 27 September 1861 that Bomar, since his promotion to sergeant, 'has never exercised his office, not having yet recovered from his severe wound.' It is probable that the surviving coat and pants were issued to him in hospital shortly before 1 October 1861, the date of his discharge because of these wounds, or were sent home to him later because they were not needed by other members of his company. Although the exact date when Porter brought the uniforms to Manassas is unknown, he was with the Legion by 6 October. Curiously, the bulk of the uniforms do not seem to have been distributed until 20-21 October.

The Bomar coat and trousers are of a greyish-brown jeans material of mixed cotton and wool, which was originally grey, as may be seen in an area once covered by the trousers stripe. The coat was based in

Turner T. Wright, Co. K, Orr's Rifles, possibly wears the brown uniform supplied to his regiment during the Fall of 1861. Alternatively it may be that worn after his transfer to Co. E, 20th South Carolina Volunteers, in which case it is representative of the six-button frock coat issued by the state quartermaster department between 1862-63. Courtesy of his great-great-grandson, Dan Snipes.

certain respects on M1851 U.S. dress regulations, and has half-inch light yellow or buff tape edging round the collar, and eight buttons on the front, which are brass eagle buttons with a 'V' on the shield, of the type made by Scovills & Co., Waterbury, Connecticut, for enlisted men of the Regular United States Army's Regiment of Voltigeurs and Foot Riflemen (1847-1848) in the Mexican War. These were attached by pushing the looped shank of each button through the coat cloth, and threading a long piece of braid through each shank. Not coincidentally, the Regiment of Voltigeurs was originally designed to be a 'legion' comprising infantry, artillery and dragoons, and to have a uniform of 'dark gray' with yellow trimming. It is possible that, following the lead of the U.S. Voltigeur Regiment, it was intended to dress the infantry, cavalry and artillery of the Hampton Legion all in the same uniform with yellow trim. In addition,

In this tinted/painted image, originally taken on 8 April 1861, Jackson Elijah Hinson wears the full dress uniform of the **Camden Light Infantry**, a volunteer militia company attached to the 22nd Regiment, South Carolina Militia. This unit went into Confederate service as the **Camden Volunteers, Co. E, 2nd South Carolina Volunteers (Kershaw's)**, which was also known as the **Palmetto Regiment**. Camden Archive.

yellow trim was appropriate for the infantry of the Legion, originally designated 'voltigeurs', because yellow had been a distinctive branch trim of the French voltigeurs and their successors, the 'chasseurs a pied', since the Napoleonic Wars.

Except in having 8 buttons rather than 9 or 10 (not a very consequential difference in Confederate uniforms), the Bomar coat matches those made earlier in 1861 at Porter's Industrial School for the 1st South Carolina Volunteers (Gregg's). The sleeves were plain without buttons or slashes. The rear skirts were divided from the waist seam down, and one pocket was set inside each skirt. Bomar's trousers were also originally grey with a light yellow or buff strip of one inch wide braid on the outer seam. In the rear was a slit some four inches long, originally held together to adjust the waist size by two four and a half-inch long straps probably once fastened by a buckle. In a style frequently found in U.S. Army officers' trousers, two 'frog pockets' in the front were fastened by small buttons.

Hampton's Legion at Seven Pines, 1862.

At Seven Pines, or Fair Oaks Station, on 31 May 1862, Hampton's Legion made at least three charges through dense woodland raked by murderous grape, canister and musketry fire. An anonymous staff officer present recalled: '...on getting to the woods our little brigade found itself unsupported within fifty yards of a heavy battery, flanked by fifteen thousand infantry, strongly entrenched.' The 363 strong Legion lost 21 killed, 118 wounded and 13 missing. This was a greater loss by far in proportion to its numbers than any other regiment in Brigadier-General W.H.C. Whiting's division.

The plate opposite depicts a private of the Washington Light Infantry Volunteers, Co. A, (left) wearing tattered remains of the frock coat and trousers issued to Hampton's Legion in October 1861. Made at the 'Industrial School for Girls' on Ashley Street, Charleston, it consisted of various shades of grey jeans material of mixed cotton and wool, trimmed with yellow or buff braid. The choice of trim colour, which was coincidentely worn by the U.S. Army Regiment of Voltigeurs and Foot Riflemen during the Mexican War, may echo Wade Hampton's original intention that the Legion infantry should

fulfil that branch of service.

A second member of the same company (right) wears a well worn collarless green flannel shirt, with two breast pockets, under which is a dirty white cotton shirt. His grey pants are the same as those worn by the first figure. Both men wear short off-white gaiters, and equipped with waist belts, shoulder belts supporting cartridge boxes, cap pouches and bayonet scabbards, and are armed with Enfield Short Pattern Rifles, cal. .577, with sabre bayonets.

The field officer (top) is based on descriptions of Major James Conner. He wears his blue militia frock coat over a red French shirt, and grey checked pants. Rank is indicated by an embroidered star on each side of the collar and red waist sash. His cap is a plain grey Model 1858 pattern, which was basically a Model 1851 dress cap with stiffening removed from all but the crown. A gold-embroidered palmetto tree graces its front. A black leather sword belt is fastened around his waist by a brass clasp bearing the palmetto device. He holds a Colt Navy Revolver, Model 1851, which he has drawn from a black leather flapped holster. Painting by Richard Hook.

When Private Hutson of the Washington Light Infantry received his regimental uniform on 20 October, he was not impressed: 'This morning we were furnished with the new uniform coats & pants, two pair of socks & two warm flannel shirts apiece. The stuff of which the coats & pants are made is wretched. They are not as warm as those we have worn through the summer.'

The 1st Regiment of Rifles, South Carolina Volunteers, (not to be confused with the similarly titled militia regiment mentioned earlier), commanded by James Lawrence Orr and organised during the summer of 1861, received a uniform based on a very specific set of regulations published in contemporary South Carolina newspapers in two slightly different versions. According to the *Keowee Courier*, of Pickens Court House, field officers were to wear dark blue double-breasted frock coats with two rows of nine buttons. The standing collar was of green velvet, edged with gilt lace. Cuffs were two and a half inches deep of solid green velvet, with two small buttons on the under seam. Coat skirts were trimmed with a one inch wide green velvet stripe. The *Abbeville Press* stipulated two rows of eight buttons. Field officers' pantaloons were also of dark blue cloth, 'made full in the legs' and trimmed with one inch wide gold lace on the outer seams. Their hats followed 1861 U.S. regulations, and were broad-brimmed black felt, six inches in the crown, with a black ostrich feather, and right side looped up by a gold cord to a small button. A gilt Palmetto Tree was specified for the side of the turned-up brim, whilst a gilt bugle horn, identifiable as the M1834 U.S. Infantry cap insignia, adorned the front of the crown.

Officers' rank insignia for Orr's Regiment of Rifles was influenced by a version of the Confederate States uniform regulations released unofficially in the Southern press during May 1861, but some chose to change them to comply with the official C.S. dress regulations issued the next month. Based on the 'leaked' version, sleeves remained plain, whilst a system of gilt stars decorated the collar. However, those officers in Orr's Regiment who did choose to follow C.S. regulations adopted the stars or bars collar insignia, but misinterpreted the wording of these regulations and placed straight gilt bars of braid running along the outside seam of the sleeve from the cuff to the elbow (two bars for captain and one for

Frock coat and trousers supplied to Robert Hayne Bomar, Washington Light Infantry Volunteers, Hampton's Legion, by the South Carolina Quartermaster Department during October 1861. Made of grey jeans cloth, they were trimmed with yellow, or buff, tape. From photographs by Ron Field.

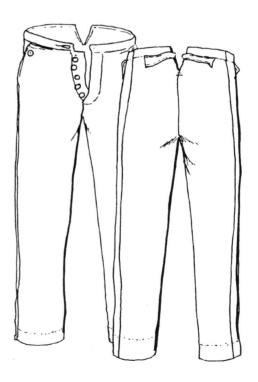

This tinted image of a South Carolinian officer is tentatively identified as Captain James M. White, Company I, 1st South Carolina Volunteers (Hagood's). Note his ornate militia staff officer's sword attached to a white leather waist belt. David Edelen.

William Zachariah Leitner was commissioned First Lieutenant of the Camden Volunteers, Co. E, 2nd South Carolina Volunteers (Kershaw's) on 9 April 1861. He rose to the rank of captain before losing his leg at Gettysburg, after which he served on the Bureau of Conscription as enrolling officer for Kershaw District. In this early war image, he wears a C.S. regulation officer's frock coat. Camden Archives.

lieutenant), simply including the number of braids but not the specified Austrian knot shape.

Staff and company officers wore single-breasted, nine-button, dark blue frock coats trimmed on collar, breast, skirt, and cuffs with green velvet. Pants were also dark blue with green seam stripes. The Surgeon and Chaplain were the exception with black seam stripes. Hats were the same as field officers. The sergeant major and quartermaster sergeant wore the same uniform as company officers, minus green trim on the coat, with gold lace chevrons on each upper arm. Sergeants, corporals and privates wore a 'Dark blue jeans' frock coat and pants trimmed in the same style as company officers with narrow green worsted braid. Non-commissioned officers' chevrons were green worsted, point down above the elbow for sergeants, 'commencing with four for the First Sergeant, and diminishing one for each Sergeant.' Corporals were worn point upwards below the elbow, 'four for the First Corporal, and diminishing one for

each Corporal.' Hats for NCOs and privates were the same as officers, minus feather, with a two-inch high gilt Palmetto Tree insignia in front, with one-inch high company letter underneath.

For fatigue dress, officers were prescribed frock coats and pants of dark blue jeans trimmed with green velvet, whilst NCOs and privates wore a 'roundabout coat', or shell jacket, of the same material trimmed with narrow green worsted braid. All ranks wore forage caps of 'Glazed silk or oil cloth.'

These uniforms were to be furnished by 'patriotic citizens' of the Districts in South Carolina from which the companies came. Furthermore, each soldier was requested to provide himself with 'a cape of oil or enamel cloth, to be fastened to the collar of the coat with three small buttons, and to extend three inches below the elbow...', plus 'one large Bowie knife, knapsacks, haversacks and canteens.'

By mid-August these uniforms were still being made up and, based on photographic evidence, many local seamstresses used grey rather than dark blue cloth, possibly influenced by C.S. regulations. Realising that this clothing would be 'much worn before mid-winter', Colonel Orr issued an appeal on 23 August 1861 for a more suitable uniform for the regiment, to consist of 'a thick heavy woollen plains or jeans coat, overcoat and pants.' The 'Ladies of Pickens, Anderson and Abbeville Districts' were advised to 'Dye the cloth brown; this you can do from the trees and shrubs of our own forests...' The skirts of these 'Dress-coats' were to extend 'to within three inches of the knee,' with 'stand-up collar, one and three fourth inches high; single-breasted;...buttons, covered with the same material of the coat.' Overcoats were to be 'double-breasted, and to button all the way up; the capes to be fastened by buttons, so that it may be removed from the coat when not needed; the skirt of the coat to extend three inches below the knee.'

The State Quartermaster Department continued to supply locally-made uniforms and clothing to South Carolinian troops until at least the end of 1864. James A. Carter, of Charleston, made up '1745 frock coats, 131 overcoats and 74 pairs of pants' during January/February 1862. From 'Horsey, Auten & Co., Charleston,' was purchased 576 'brown round-crown felt hats, 840 brown square-crown, 672 black round-crown and 792 black square-crown' on 8 January 1862. Earlier, during July 1861, the department had paid Porter's Industrial School 'for Making 50 Inft Uniforms' which indicates that some kind of branch service system was in effect - possibly using black or dark blue trim for infantry, yellow for cavalry, and red for artillery. The cloth used by the Quartermaster Department at Charleston for coats and pants included 'Cadet Jeans', 'Grey Woolens', 'Grey Satinet', 'Steel mix'd Tweeds' and 'Brown Plains'. Shirts appear to have been made from 'Striped Osnaburgs', 'Algonquin Twilled Stripes', 'Troy Cottonade', 'Checked Cottonade' and a variety of cotton plaids.

Returns exist for clothing received and issued at the Quartermaster Department at Columbia, the state capital, for the periods 1 June through 31 December 1862, and for the entire year of 1864. The most interesting is a monthly return for 1 June 1862, listing 8024 'Unif. Coats', 4107 'Pants', 2361 'O'Coats', 127 'Woolen Capes', 645 'Grey Caps', and 90 'Hats'. Very little clothing was issued from Columbia during the third quarter of 1862, but from October to December 1862 were issued 7957 coats, 3772 pairs of pants, 2518 overcoats, 1469 cotton drawers, 531 flannel shirts, 48

Henry Bryson Nickles enlisted as a private in Company F of the infantry battalion, Holcombe Legion, during the summer of 1861. He wears a plain frock coat with collar turned down, possibly of state quartermaster manufacture. His waist belt has been reversed, with buckle at his back, in order to compensate for the 'mirror image' effect of the original ambrotype. S.C. Confederate Relic Room & Museum.

tweed shirts, 196 hickory shirts, 645 caps and 22 hats. These items were probably being transferred to Virginia for distribution to South Carolina soldiers in the Army of Northern Virginia. By 1864 the state was not issuing any clothing in Columbia except a few shoes.

The state issuance of 1862-63 appears to have consisted a slightly longer grey frock coat than that of 1861. It had only six (sometimes seven) buttons. Commonly the collar was trimmed with tape or cord forming the edging and a false buttonhole, and the pointed cuffs were trimmed in the same style, sometimes topped with an oval loop. Some had a solid branch-colour collar and cuffs, while others may have been completely plain. Trousers continued to be grey with one inch-wide branch-colour seam stripes. Headgear appears to have been 'cadet-pattern' forage caps, either grey or (in early 1862) dark blue, to which

This heavily tinted/painted image is of Private Henry F. Dominick, Co. H, Holcombe Legion infantry battalion. Dominick enlisted on 17 November 1863 and died of fever on 31 July 1864 at Stoney Creek, Virginia. S.C. Confederate Relic Room & Museum.

Private John Bagnal Brogdon enlisted in the cavalry battalion of the Holcombe Legion on 13 November 1861. He had a horse valued at $225 and equipment worth $25. For reasons unknown he was discharged five weeks later. Hence his eight-button plain grey frock coat may be identified to a specific period of issue. Note his oval 'SC' belt plate. He grips a derringer-type pistol in right hand, and a U.S. Model 1840 sabre, or Palmetto Armory copy, in his left. S.C. Confederate Relic Room & Museum.

brass company and regimental numbers and letters were sometimes attached. The six-button frock coat was superceded by a six-button shell jacket, with or without branch-service colour trim, which was being issued by mid-1863. The collar 'buttonhole' was omitted from this jacket, and all other trimming was often omitted. The possible successor to this pattern was the plain five-button jacket issued by the Confederate Clothing Depot in Charleston by 1864.

Mississippi

Following the secession of Mississippi on 9 January 1861, the State Convention established a state military force called the Army of Mississippi, and a Military Board consisting of Governor John J. Pettus and five generals which, sometime during March 1861, published 'Orders' for the organization and maintenance of this force. Included within these orders were detailed uniform regulations, which were subsequently

Unidentified enlisted man in a uniform based on that prescribed for the Army of Mississippi. His coat is fastened by gilt Mississippi 'star'-pattern buttons. Mississippi Department of Archives & History.

reprinted as part of the 'Southern Military Manual', published in both Jackson and New Orleans, which contained the collected 'military ordinances' of Mississippi and Louisiana.

The Army of Mississippi, according to the orders of the Military Board, was to consist of a division of eight regiments of infantry or riflemen, ten companies of cavalry and ten of artillery. Unlike other seceded states who formed small 'regular' full-time state forces, the Army of Mississippi was not conceived as such. After mustering in, the men were furloughed and recalled for training when required. By mid-March, nearly forty companies had been formed into the 1st-8th Infantry Regiments, within four brigades. Many of these were existing volunteer militia companies, and since less than two years previously a militia act had attempted to organize the volunteer militia of the state into a division, it is difficult to understand why the 1861 Military Board should have wanted to duplicate this organization. As other volunteer militia companies were mustered into the Provisional Army of the Confederate States during 1861, the Army of Mississippi was by-passed. When some of the latter's commands did go into 'camp of instruction' late in the year, complaints of wasted resources were heard. The eight infantry regiments were disbanded in January 1862, whilst the cavalry and artillery seem not to have materialised.

The uniform for the Army of Mississippi was prescribed in detail. For full dress, grey frock coats were to be of U.S. regulation cut, although all double-breasted coats, for generals as well as field officers, bore two rows of seven buttons. Generals' cuffs were plain, but their collars were of black velvet, with an embroidered $3/4$ inch gilt star each side for the Major-General, and silver stars for Brigadiers. Field officers wore black cloth collars minus the star, and black cuffs, all edged with $1/2$ inch gold lace. Staff officers' coats were not braided. Company officers had collars and cuffs of branch service colour, and horizontal silk braid

of the same colour running across from their nine buttons, the top braids being five inches in length, and the bottom two. Enlisted mens' coats were similar, but with worsted braid. Branch service colour was to be crimson for infantry and riflemen, yellow for cavalry, and orange for artillery.

Trousers were also grey, with black cord stripes for generals, and one inch cloth stripes for the rest, black for field officers, and of branch service colour for the remainder. Hats were of black felt, broad brimmed and 'looped up on three sides,'with cord, tassel and plume for parade. The plume was to be 'long flowing'

Unidentified officer in the uniform prescribed by the Military Board for the Army of Mississippi in March 1861. Mississippi Department of Archives & History.

for generals, field and staff officers, and 'short and standing' for all other ranks. Plume colours were - white for Major General, red tipped white for Brigadier-General, crimson for regimental field and staff, green for the Medical Corps, yellow for the Adjutant General's Corps, blue for the Quartermaster General's department, and blue tipped with red for the Ordnance Corps. Captains, lieutenants and enlisted

The Jeff Davis Rifles, of Holly Springs, enlisted into Confederate service as Co. D, 9th Mississippi Infantry. They paraded at Pensacola, Florida, for photographer J. D. Edwards wearing their pre-war full dress uniform consisting of grey tail coats and M1851 dress caps. Mississippi Department of Archives & History.

men wore plumes of the colour of the 'facings of their dress.' Yellow metal regimental numbers were to be worn below the plume socket for Regimental Field and Staff officers. These were probably substituted for company letters for Captain and all other ranks. Cords and tassels were to be gold for all officers, and worsted facing colour for other ranks.

Officers' rank was to be indicated by a system of dark blue shoulder straps with gold borders. Like their full dress epaulettes, these bore a rank system consisting of a gold star for Major General, silver star for Brigadier General, gold crescent for Colonel, gold leaf for Lieutenant Colonel, silver leaf for major, two gold bars for Captain, one for First Lieutenant, and none for Second and Third lieutenants. Non-commissioned officers' chevrons were basically as per U.S. regulations, in facing colours, of silk for Sergeant-Major, Quartermaster Sergeant, and Ordnance Sergeant; of worsted for 1st Sergeant and below.

For fatigue, enlisted men were to wear flannel shirts with a white star on each side of the collar. Those for infantry and riflemen were to be red, grey for artillery, and blue for cavalry.

After these orders were issued, the Military Board apparently had second thoughts about the unusual, and possibly confusing, branch service colours prescribed. On 14 March 1861, the New Orleans *Daily Delta* reported: 'Mississippi regulation uniform (grey) changed by the Military Board to Infantry and Light Infantry ... Green, Artillery ... Red, Cavalry ... Yellow or Orange.'

However, in a final version of the regulations, these colours were changed yet again. This was included as part of the collected 'military ordinances' of Mississippi in the 'Southern Military Manual', a handbook for officers published simultaneously in Mississippi and Louisiana, probably in May 1861. Here the facing colours were given as blue for infantry and riflemen, orange for cavalry, and red for artillery, while fatigue shirts were now grey for infantry, blue for cavalry, and red for artillery.

While there is considerable doubt that many Mississippi companies wore any of the three prescribed versions of these uniform regulations in their entirety, it is likely that they served as a partial guide for the war companies subsequently organized. A number of companies chose to wear three-cornered hats and/or coats with horizontal bars of trim on their chests. The Alcorn Rifles, Co. F, and the James Creek Volunteers, Co. H, 1st Mississippi Infantry, are both recorded as wearing horizontal bars on their coats. The Ben Bullard Rifles, Co. B, 10th Mississippi Infantry, were photographed by J.D. Edwards manning heavy artillery at Pensacola in late April or early May 1861, wearing a uniform based almost in every detail on that prescribed by the State Military Board. Henry Augustus Moore of the Water Valley Rifle Guard, Co. F, 15th Mississippi Infantry, wore a grey coat with short one inch-wide bars across the chest. Sinclair B. Carter of the Choctaw Guards, Co. I, 15th Mississippi wore horizontal bars on his coat which appear to have been connected by two sets of short ties, thus securing the coat at the front. Both coats had solid branch service-coloured collar and cuffs. The Lamar Rifles, Co. G, 11th Mississippi Infantry, wore grey frock coats with eight chest bars terminating with buttons at either end. Their hats were pinned up on one side only, and were adorned with infantry bugle horn insignia and, in some cases, a single black ostrich feather. The Natchez Fencibles, Co. G, 12th Mississippi Infantry, wore the same type of coat. The Jeff Davis Rifles, Co. D, 9th Mississippi Infantry, also wore thin bars of trim with buttons at either end on their grey tail coats. Regarding the last two units, descretion should be observed concerning their uniforms, as they were both organised prior to 1860, and formed part of the 2nd Regiment, 1st Brigade, of the Volunteer Militia established in May 1860. As such, they may be wearing a company uniform adopted before the State regulations of 1861.

Three identified photographs survive of Mississippi soldiers wearing three-cornered hats. Thomas M. Barr of the Quitman Guards, Co. E, 16th Missisippi Infantry, and Thomas P. Gooch of the Carroll Guards, Co.C, 20th Mississippi Infantry, both had the popular large white metal star pinning up one side of their hats. William F. Parks of the Confederate Guard, Co. G, 17th Mississippi Infantry, was photographed holding a hat pinned up on at least two sides.

Regarding fatigue shirts, Frederick LeCand of the Natchez Fencibles was photographed wearing an example of that prescribed by the 'Manual'. Light grey in colour, it had a small dark blue five-pointed star embroidered on either side of the turned down collar, thus combining elements of the original fatigue regulations prescribed by the Military Board. Other more elaborately-trimmed shirt types were worn

minus the collar star. That chosen by the True Confederates, Co. C, 8th Mississippi Infantry, was typical, consisting of a light grey shirt buttoning all the way down the front, with dark blue trim on collar, along shoulders, around pocket and sleeves, and either side of the buttons.

The Bolivar Troop, Co. H, 1st Battalion of Mississippi Cavalry, adopted a grey pull-over woollen shirt with trim, possibly dark blue in colour, on front, collar and around the sleeves. Their pants varied in colour, with broad seam stripes. Hats were grey felt with low crown and three inch-wide brim pinned up on the right side with a star-shaped insignia. They were decorated with black ostrich feather plume, and had a wide silk band to which was fastened the brass letters 'BT'. The Natchez Cavalry, Co. A, 2nd Battalion of Mississippi Cavalry, also wore a grey shirt with one inch-wide trim around collar, cuffs, down the

A member of the Natchez Fencibles, Co. B, 12th Mississippi Infantry (left), wearing a fatigue shirt patterned after that originally prescribed by the Military Board for the Army of Mississippi. Two further versions of fatigue shirts worn by Mississippi volunteers. The Shubuta Rifles, Co. A, 14th Mississippi Infanty (centre); and the Quitman Guards, Co. E, 16th Mississippi Infantry (right). Based on photographs by Ron Field.

According to the 'Minute Book' of the Smith-Quitman Rifles of Jackson, who volunteered for sixty days' service in the 3rd Regiment State Troops during September 1861, they chose to wear a grey woollen shirt trimmed with half inch-wide green braid around the collar, cuffs and across the top of each chest pocket, with two stripes up the front from the waist to the neck. Their pants were of 'Blue cottonade' with half inch-wide green worsted braid down the outside seam. Hats were 'Black felt, crown six inches high, three-inch brim - with left side hooked up - and fastened with [a] Large Military button.' This uniform was described as being based on that worn by the Burt Rifles, Co. K, 18th Mississippi Infantry, with 'some slight alterations.' From descriptions by Ron Field.

buttoned front, and along the top of slanting pockets. Two members of the Confederate Guards, an artillery company organised in Pontotoc County in 1861, were photographed wearing grey cotton over-shirts and pants with dark, probably red, facings and seam stripes, and light grey tricorne hats.

Numerous Mississippi companies volunteered for Confederate service in uniforms which owed nothing to the regulations of 1861. The Mississippi Rifles, Co. A, 10th Mississippi Infantry, wore a dress uniform described in 1860 as being 'of dark green cloth, Hungarian hats, ostrich plumes.' The collar, worsted epaulettes and cuff tabs on their single-breasted frock coats were red, as was their trouser stripes. Their 'Hardee'-style dress hat bore a red ostrich plume and was pinned up on the right by a regulation US eagle; on the front was a Mounted Rifles-style bugle, placed horizontally, over large metal letters 'MR'. During February 1861, this company acquired a fatigue uniform consisting of a seven-button grey coat with dark facings on collar, pointed cuffs and shoulder straps, plain grey pants and a grey cap with dark band. The Van Dorn Reserves, of Aberdeen, were mustered into service as Co. I, 11th Mississippi Infantry, in a uniform of 'red jeans.' The Prairie Guards, Co. E of the same regiment, originally wore a dress uniform consisting of grey frock coat with dark-coloured plastron front and epaulettes, grey pants with broad seam stripes, and black Hardee hat with ostrich plume and brim looped up on the left. A member of this company later informed his parents that he had sold his 'red jeans pants for four dollars', possibly indicating that more than one company of this regiment was thus clad for war service.

Predominantly an agricultural state with very few facilities to process cloth, Mississippi was virtually destitute of all supplies by February 1861. The government slowly realised that in order to provide clothing for their troops they would have to take stringent action. By the summer of 1861, it virtually monopolised the state's textile industry, and had directed that all penitentiary labour be, as far as possible, employed in producing supplies for the soldiers of Mississippi. The prison workshops had been established in the Mississippi State Penitentiary at Jackson in 1849. By 1860, this facility consisted of 2,304 spindles, 24 cotton-carding machines, 76 looms for weaving osnaburgs, 4 mills for producing cotton twills, and a full complement of machinery for making woollen linseys and cotton batting. When Mississippi belatedly began to arm after secession, the entire penitentiary facilities were diverted to the manufacture of military goods. The extent of its services to the state's war effort can be gauged from the fact that its output during the last twelve months of its existence (July 1862 to July 1863) was reckoned at $172,608.

The 'Mississippi Manufacturing Company', established in 1848 by James Wesson near Drane's Mill, in Choctaw County, was the state's second largest textile factory, with 1,000 cotton spindles, 500 woollen spindles, 20 looms, and a large wool-carding machine. The factory's labour force consisted of 85 well-trained white mill workers, who were comfortably housed in homes provided for them in the company-owned village of Bankston. The isolation of the Bankston

factory, chosen originally to keep the labour force away from the temptations of the city 'grog shops', later paid unexpected dividends. Hostile Federal cavalry did not chance upon it until almost a year after the state's more accessible factories had been burned to the ground during the Vicksburg campaign of 1863. According to a letter written to Governor John J. Pettus by Wesson, this Company had by the beginning of August 1861 provided samples and prices of cloth for uniforms, and was investigating the cost of dying on a large scale. Other textile mills turned over to wartime production included the 'Green factory' on

John LeRoy Williams of the Sardis Blues, Co. F, 12th Mississippi Infantry, wears a plain grey fatigue shirt, and is armed with a M1842 Musket and hunting knife. Note the large frame buckle on his waist belt. Massachusetts Commandery Military Order of the Loyal Legion & the U.S. Army Military History Institute/photo by Jim Enos.

the Pearl River in Jackson County, and 'Wilkinson Manufacturing Company' at Woodville in Wilkinson County.

It is difficult to ascertain exactly what type of uniforms these establishments produced for the men

First Lieutenant Israel Spencer, Issaquena Artillery, Captain Rice E. Grave's Company, Mississippi Artillery. His cap has an unusually-shaped cross cannon insignia patch, which may have been red, in keeping with branch service colour. Alice F. Sage Collection, USAMHI.

Unidentified member of the Moody True Blues, Co. D, 8th Mississippi Infantry. Raised in Clarke County, Mississippi, most of this unit was wiped at the battle of Murfreesboro on 31 December 1862. David Wynn Vaughan collection.

who volunteered for service in mid-1861. The Satartia Rifles who were mustered-in as Co. I, 12th Mississippi Infantry, during April wore very neat nine-button grey frock coats with dark trim around collar, shoulder straps and cuffs. Pants and hats were plain grey. The Long Creek Rifles, Co. A, 15th Mississippi Infantry, adopted plain grey frock coats, grey pants trimmed with wide black seam stripes, and black felt hats.

Mississippi regiments in Virginia were very poorly supplied. According to the diary of Robert A. Moore, a member of the Confederate Guards, camped near Leesburg, Virginia, during August 1861, the 17th Mississippi Infantry purchased 'for the Reg.[iment] goods for a uniform' which was taken 'back to the homes of the different companies' to be made up. Received by the end of October, these uniforms consisted of grey ten-button shell jackets with a single small button on either side of a black trimmed collar. Cuffs were decorated with black cord forming a distinctive single loop. The front and bottom jacket edges were also trimmed with black cord. Some jackets had a single pocket on the right breast. Pants were also grey with two-inch wide seam stripes.

As 1861 drew to a close, the lack of clothing began to affect the Mississippi troops closer to home. The 1st and 3rd Mississippi were described as 'the poorest clad, shod and armed body I ever saw,' by Brigadier-General Floyd Tilghman, commanding Camp Alcorn in Kentucky on 2 November of that year. Though widespread, this shortage was not general. One survivor of the 2nd Mississippi Infantry, often reported as one of the worst dressed regiments, recalled 1861 as a time of plenty. Much of this clothing was paid for and supplied by 'volunteer aid societies' of Mississippi.

Florida

Nicknamed the 'smallest tadpole' in the Confederacy, Florida seceded from the Union on 10 January 1861. However, her war preparations had begun months earlier. Independent companies of 'Minute Men' were formed during 1860, and late that year began to offer their services to the state, thereby supplementing its small number of volunteer militia units. Raised and equipped almost entirely by private means, these new companies were speedily accepted into state service by Governor Madison S. Perry. A reorganisation of the dormant beat militia system, consisting of twenty-one regiments arranged in two divisions, was also begun by an act of legislature on 14 February 1861. This called

William G. Denham was still a West Florida Seminary Cadet when this ambrotype was taken in 1861. He enlisted in the Leon Rifles, Co. A, 1st Florida Infantry, soon after. The unusual multi-pointed star insignia on his belt plate may be specific to his military school. Florida State Archives.

Private Walter Miles Parker of Co. H, 1st Florida Cavalry, was photographed on enlistment wearing this uniform, which his commanding officer acquired via a Virginia contractor in 1861. His light grey six-button sack coat, with patch sewn along the shoulders, may indicate a North Carolina provenance. This regiment served as infantry before leaving Florida in Spring 1862. Florida State Archives, used with permission of Richard J. Ferry.

This unidentified man in a fatigue shirt enlisted in the Trapier Guard, Co. C, 5th Florida Infantry. Note the reversed letters 'TG' on his belt plate. USAMHI/photo by Jim Enos.

James Alfred Stephens, South Florida Infantry, Co. B, 7th Florida Infantry, wears the well-made shell jacket and pants he received after enlistment in April 1862. Note the light-coloured piping on his cap. Florida State Archives.

for an immediate enrollment of all able bodied men and their organisation into companies and regiments. Consequently, the Governor was immediately authorised to raise two regiments of infantry and one of cavalry or mounted riflemen for six-month state service. This was later supplemented by two more cavalry regiments, two battalions of State Guards, and a number of independent companies of artillery, mounted riflemen and infantry.

In response to the call of the Confederate War Department on 9 March 1861 for 500 men to garrison Pensacola, the state raised the 1st Florida Infantry which was largely composed of existing companies. Subsequent calls on 8 and 16 April led to the formation of the 2nd Florida Infantry, sent to Virginia, and the 3rd and 4th Regiments, which were initially used to defend the Florida coast line. Eventually, Florida provided some 15,000 troops for the Confederacy, which were organised into twelve infantry regiments, two cavalry regiments, and seven independent companies of light artillery.

There were no state dress regulations and no regimental uniforms in Florida until 1861. As with other states, volunteer militia companies wore a variety of individual dress uniforms, which would have been replaced by fatigue uniforms for active service. On 8 February, an act was passed empowering the Governor 'to adopt a State Uniform, which shall be distinctive in character, with such variations for the different grades and arms of service as may be appropriate.' Nothing is known regarding the design of this uniform. It appears that the supply of clothing to the new regiments came from various sources. The companies entering the 1st Florida Infantry (the Magnolia Regiment) appear to have worn militia clothing, or whatever civilian groups at home could supply in the way of service dress. Private William Denham of the Leon Rifles, Co. A of that regiment, wore a nine-button light grey shell jacket, light grey pants with narrow seam stripes, and a light-coloured forage cap, when he enlisted at Warrington in June 1861. The 2nd Florida Infantry were uniformed in cloth purchased by a combination of state and county

funding, and made into garments by several ladies' societies. The 1st Florida Cavalry hoped for the same support; when that failed its commanding officer, Lieutenant-Colonel William Davis, on his own responsibility, contracted with Baldwin & Williams, of Richmond, Virginia, to supply a coat, two pairs of pants, two shirts and an overcoat for each of his men - 1,000 suits in all.

Private Mathew A. Beck of the Gulf Coast Rangers, an Independent Company of Volunteers commanded by Captain John Chambers, which later became Co. A, 9th Florida Infantry, wore a substan-

This soldier has been tentatively identified as Theophilus S. Luckie, Co. B, 6th Florida Infantry. He wears a further example of the type of uniforms acquired out-of-state by Florida authorities. His shell jacket is remarkably similar to those worn by many Georgia units, and may have come from a Savannah or Columbus supplier. Under his kepi he wears a 'Sicilian'-style stocking cap popular with early war volunteers throughout the **South.** USAMHI/photo by Jim Enos.

tially-made nine-button plain grey frock coat.

The cloth for these various types of uniform could not be produced in the state, so agents followed the

Sergeant William R. Barineau enlisted in the Young Guards, Co. B, 8th Florida Infantry, in 1862 and went on to be killed at the Wilderness in May 1864. USAMHI/photo by Jim Enos.

It is difficult to believe that William D. Rogers wore this uniform when he was transferred to the Simpson Mounted Rangers, Co. E, 15th Confederate Cavalry, in early 1864! Note the brass letters 'SMR' on his hat, and the very elaborate system of buttons and trim on his two-tone coat. John Segreat & Florida State Archives

lead of 1st Florida Cavalry and scoured the South for supplies. Main centres visited were New Orleans, Louisiana; Savannah and Columbus, Georgia; Mobile, Alabama; and Charleston, South Carolina. The latter city was visited in June 1861 by agent James Banks, who bid against agents from other states and private concerns for cloth brought through the blockade, or made in the South itself. The Palatka Guard, a volunteer militia company commanded by Captain A.F. Braham, negotiated directly with Charleston tailor C. F. Jackson to have uniforms made up for sixty men. Regarding the styles of uniform, a member of the Marion Light Artillery wrote in May 1861: 'Captain Powell intends visiting Atlanta... for the purpose of purchasing uniforms... Our uniform consists of cadet grey or if not[,] the cloth is left to the discretion of Captain Powell... failing this he intends to purchase flannel shirts and cheap pants.'

It took until November 1861 for the legislature to authorise the state's Quartermaster General to arrange a supply of clothing for all her soldiers. According to photographs taken in early 1862, this clothing consisted of grey shell jackets and pants. A number of jackets had various combinations of exterior pockets on the chest. Trim, where used, varied according to regimental or company choice. Jackets without pockets were also supplied to units organised that year.

Alabama

After secession on 11 January 1861, the 'Republic of Alabama' existed for almost a month before she joined the Confederacy. Military preparations had been underway for fully a year prior to this step as, on 24 February 1860, an act of legislature was passed creating the 'Volunteer Corps of the State of Alabama', more usually called the 'Alabama Volunteer Corps'.

Organised under the authority of a State Military Commission, this Corps was limited in numbers to 8,150 officers and men who were carefully divided among the several counties. The old uniformed volunteer militia companies of the state were encouraged to join it, and moves were made to purchase arms. A substantial number of new volunteer companies were raised during the second half of 1860, but it is not clear to what extent the Corps absorbed them. On 15 January 1861, four days after secession, a bill called 'An Act for the Organisation of the Army of Alabama' formed a stepping stone towards the final issuance of General Order No. 1, on 28 March 1861, which described the regulation uniform devised by the State Military Commission for the Alabama Volunteer Corps. All companies were expected to adopt this

The Independent Blues of Selma, Alabama. Photographed in January 1861 wearing the uniform of the Alabama Volunteer Corps. Alabama Department of Archives & History.

J. F. Gaines of the Montgomery Mounted Rifles. This unit appears to a have preferred the Hardee hat with their Alabama Volunteer Corps uniform. Alabama Dept. of Archives & History.

Joseph Skinner wears the uniform adopted by the Mobile Rifle Guard, a company of the 1st Regiment, Alabama Militia, in April 1861. This included a grey frock coat with a twelve-button front, and broad trim on collar, shoulders, and cuffs. Note the letters 'MRG' on his kepi. Eleanor S. Brockenbrough Library, The Museum of the Confederacy, Richmond, Virginia.

garb, but were given until 1 January 1862 to comply, by which time Alabama grey clothing predominated. The Alabama Volunteer Corps as a distinctive organisation was abolished in November 1861, after which time its units were disbanded or mustered into active service.

The uniform adopted for the Alabama Volunteer Corps by the State Military Commission basically consisted of a dark blue frock coat and cadet grey pants. Officers' coats had a skirt extending two-thirds to three-quarters from the top of the hip to the bend of the knee, and were double-breasted for those above the rank of captain with buttons arranged as per U.S. Army regulations. Solid collar and parallel cuffs were trimmed with dark blue velvet and trousers were plain grey without seam stripes. Company-grade officers wore a nine-button, single-breasted coat with collar and pointed cuffs supposedly trimmed as per branch of service e.g. light blue for infantry, scarlet for artillery, emerald green for riflemen, and orange for dragoons. Trimmings consisted of a .375" band of lace around the standing collar, and pointed cuff edges. Some

company-grade officers' coats were tailored without trim. Officers' one-quarter inch wide pants seam stripes were white for infantry, and branch colours for the others. Headgear was patterned on the M1853 United States Military Academy dress cap, which consisted of a black felt body reinforced with leather. Smaller in the crown than in the band, it sloped slightly forward, with black leather crown, head band, chin-strap, and visor. Judging from photographs it was given a round pompon above a national 'eagle' of brass; below these were attached the letters 'AVC' in a slight curve. Buttons for cap and uniform bore the letters 'AVC' over the U.S. national eagle. These buttons were made in some quantity by Lambert and Mast of Philadelphia; and Horstmann and Allen of New York. Distinctive 'AVC' waist belt and cartridge box plates based on U.S. Army regulation size were also made. These were supplemented by the plain brass militia type simply engraved with the initials

2nd Volunteer Regiment, Alabama Militia, 1860-61. Officer, Auburn Guards (left): black shako with white feather plume tipped red, brass 'AG' in wreath on front; dark blue coatee with three rows of brass buttons; gold epaulettes; gold or white trim on edge of collar and cuffs. Dark blue pants with gold or white stripe; white shoulder belt; and red sash. Officer, Tuskegee Light Infantry (second from left): dark blue kepi with gold trim and wreathed 'TLI' insignia; dark blue frock coat, single row of brass buttons; gold epaulettes; gold or light blue trim on collar and cuffs; dark blue pants with gold or light blue seam stripe. Officer, Alabama Zouaves (centre): dark blue frock coat with gold lace trim on collar, cuffs, edge of coat, and chest bars; gold epaulettes; medium blue pants with gold seam stripe; blue kepi with gold braid; and red sash. Private, Montgomery True Blues (second from right): black shako with brass front plate; red feather plume; dark blue coatee with brass buttons and red facings on collar and cuffs; red epaulettes; dark blue pants with red stripe; white cross belts; and black waist belt. Musician, Montgomery True Blues (right): dark blue Mexican War-style forage cap with red band; dark blue jacket with brass buttons and red collar and cuffs; white pants. From photographs and descriptions by Ron Field. Confederate Historical Society.

Although the unit Private John T. Davis served in is not known, he probably wears the uniform adopted by Alabama in August **1861.** USAMHI/photo by Jim Enos.

This unidentified member of the Clark County Rangers, Co. D, 2nd Alabama Infantry ('The Magnolia Regiment') has 'Fight with us and end it' inscribed on his sabre, which may have been a photographer's prop. David Wynn Vaughan collection.

'AVC'.

The coat worn by enlisted men was similar to that of company grade officers, except that the length of the skirt was 'between the hip and the knee.' Trim was the same as that specified for company-grade officers. Pants' seam stripes were one and a quarter-inch wide white lace in corresponding branch colour.

With minor differences regarding insignia and pattern, this garb was widely adopted by the volunteer militia of Alabama, plus the 1st Artillery Battalion, and the 1st and 2nd Volunteer Infantry Regiments, composed mainly of newly recruited companies. More often than not the dress cap gave way to a cloth forage cap or felt hat within these units. Indeed, the state puchased 10,000 black felt hats with brims 'looped & buttoned on the left side', from R. & A. Cain of North Port, Alabama. Many officers tended to wear the Hardee hat. The unpopularity of the frock coat in certain quarters may be gauged by remarks in a letter written by Captain S.F. Nunnelee, a veteran riflemen of the Mexican War, and now in command of the

Eutaw Rifle Company, who wrote to Governor A.B. Moore on 6 September 1860: 'The prescribed uniform is the same for the whole corps - the Rifle movement is different from that of any other branch of the service. Its movements are very rapid, and carrying the gun in the right hand, the frock coat will interfere very materially with the proper handling of the piece.' Despite such reservations, many individual companies were happy to wear it. These included the Perote Guards, Pioneer Guards, Alabama Rifles, Camden Rifles, Tuskegee Light Infantry, Montgomery Mounted Rifles, and the Independent Blues. At regimental level, the 1st Regiment of Volunteer Infantry was presented with a uniform of blue 'frock shirts' buttoned down the front, blue jean pants, and wide-brimmed black hats by 'the ladies of Alabama' in July 1861. Meanwhile, T.C. DeLeon, a clerk in the Confederate topographical office in Richmond, had noted in late June, 'the Alabamians from the coast [the 8th and 9th Volunteer Infantry] nearly all in blue of a cleaner hue and neater cut' than troops from other states.

The influence of the Alabama Volunteer Corps uniform lasted well into the conflict. The 4th Volunteer Infantry were described as wearing 'dark blue jean Frock coats at Island No. 10' in 1862. During July 1863, Sergeant Crawford Jackson of the 6th Volunteer Infantry reported he was wearing 'a black broad cloth coat, Alabama staff buttons, cut and trimmed in regulation style, a pair of grey trousers and slouch hat...'

Another uniform issuance, known as the 'Alabama State Uniform', was also prescribed by Governor Moore during February 1861 for those units not called into Confederate service. This was described as follows: 'The coat, pants and cap of regimental officers and enlisted men called into service of the State of Alabama ... will be cadet grey. The trimmings, badges of rank and pattern of uniform will be the same as that of the United States Army, conforming to same colors to distinguished corps.' A report from Mobile shortly thereafter, describing 'Alabama volunteers in homespun coarse grey suits, with blue and yellow facings and stripes,' may be a reference to this uniform.

Not all Alabamian companies adopted these prescribed uniforms. One officer informed the Governor that his company had bought uniforms which he feared might 'differ from the State Uniform.' He went to explain that it was 'like the Dutchman's Wife: not much for pretty, but Hell for strong.' A report from Montgomery on 28 April 1861 mentioned encountering 'uniforms of every variety and every stripe.' This was particularly the case with the older

Sergeant William Henry Phillips is believed to have enlisted in the Pickens Stars, a unit designated Co. E, 40th Alabama Infantry. The brass letters 'CG' on his gold-braided cap may indicate that he belonged to another company, such as the Creagh Guards or the Clifton Guards, of Alabama. USAMHI/ photo by Jim Enos.

volunteer militia companies who continued to wear elements of their dress uniforms supplemented by items of service wear. That of the Mobile Cadets consisted of a grey forage cap with black band, nine-button grey jacket with collar, cuffs and shoulder straps faced black with white piping, and grey pants with light-coloured (possibly gold) seam stripes. Setting aside their 'Continental uniform', the State Artillery wore a 'handsome service uniform of indigo blue trimmed with red, and brown gaiters' in May 1861. The Perote Guards adopted a fatigue dress including a coat of 'very dark cassimere, heavy weight, trimmed with light gray, single row of buttons and frock skirts.' The Emerald Guards of Mobile initially wore green frock coats, but later adopted an eight-button grey satinette or broadcloth shell jacket with dark (possibly green) facings on collar and cuffs, and very light-coloured pants.

Some of the newly-formed companies also adopted

very individual, locally-made garb. A reporter in Montgomery noted that many Alabama volunteers wore: '...old flannel bags, closed and drawn to a point at one end, with tassel dependent. This style of fatigue head-dress was introduced by one of the Mobile Companies, and in an incredibly short space of time the fever for possessing them spread from rank to rank, and Company to Company, until nearly everyone now is supplied.'

This head-dress was the 'Sicilian' cap, made famous by the Sicilian revolutionaries led by Giuseppe Garibaldi in 1860. The Raccoon Roughs, Co. I, 6th Alabama Infantry, proudly sported rough fur caps made of raccoon skins when they marched off in May 1861. The Dale County Beauregards, Co. E, 15th Alabama Infantry, wore a uniform of white osnaburg with 'blue stripes on the trousers and jackets.' The Henry Pioneers, Co. G of the same regiment, went to war in red flannel shirts. Hardaway's Artillery acquired 'coarse gray tunics with yellow facings, & French caps.'

Although the state supplied some of the clothing for these uniforms, by mid-April 1861 it found itself unable to cope with the growing number of companies rapidly forming. It therefore handed over responsibility to the Confederate government which was in no position to supply clothing, but promised financial support via the commutation system. Three months later, it became apparent that the Alabama troops in Confederate service were being poorly outfitted, and that little provision was being made for the coming winter. Once again the state assumed responsibility for clothing and equipping its men in the field, as well as the new companies being formed, by collecting commutation money from the Confederacy or from the men themselves. Hence Governor Moore issued a circular on 26 August 1861 emphasizing that the items most needed were: 'Uniform jackets, great coats and pantaloons of good strong cloth, of gray color ... shirts of flannel, or checked or striped cotton; draws of woolen, or cotton flannel or stout osnaburgs; woolen socks; gloves, shoes and blankets.'

On 31 August, the Quartermaster General, Brigadier General Duff C. Green, announced in the *Montgomery Weekly Advertiser* that the proposed uniform was to consist of a single-breasted seven-button jacket with low standing collar and pocket inside the left breast. Straps were attached to the shoulders, and five inch-long belt loops sewn on the bottom of the jacket on the side seams. Pantaloons were to be cut full. The great coat also had a standing collar, and was fastened by seven large brass military buttons. The cape reached to the elbow with five small buttons on the right, and was removeable and fastened to the collar with six hooks and eyes.

Because these uniforms were to be made by numerous soldiers' aid societies, as well as large textile companies, an attempt was made to ensure that a reasonable level of uniformity was achieved by sending out clothing patterns together with available samples. To obtain cloth, buttons and other materials, the state entered into contracts with firms including the Eagle Manufacturing Company of Columbus, Georgia; the Prattville Manufacturing Company of Prattville, Alabama; Phillips, Fariss and Company of Montgomery, Alabama; and Barnett Micon and Company of Tallassee, Alabama. The first three firms supplied 56,300 yards of hickory shirting, linsey, kersey and drilling, while the last mentioned provided 1010 grey and white blankets, and 14,000 military buttons.

The collective response to Governor Moore's appeal was considerable. By the end of 1861 the following had been furnished: 7,416 complete uniforms, 2,974 great coats, 2,412 blankets and 3,000 pairs of shoes. During the first quarter of 1862, ninety soldiers' aid societies and suppliers had contributed over 1,532 uniforms, 900 great coats, 1,644 pairs of pants, 3,810 flannel, cotton and hickory shirts, and 1,082 pairs of shoes. Each piece of completed uniform was marked according to its size by a numbered card firmly sewn to the garment. Each item was boxed and shipped to either Huntsville or Montgomery at the expense of the state. They were then directed to Governor Moore for distribution. Typical of issuance via this source was that of the Calhoun Guards, Co. A, 2nd Alabama Infantry, who, whilst camped at Fort Morgan, Alabama, received from 'the state of Alabama before being mustered into the service of the Confederate States of America...: 72 common caps, 72 uniform coats, 72 overalls, 144 flannel shirts, 144 pairs of drawers, 144 pairs of socks, 72 blankets, [and] 144 undershirts.'

A member of Captain A. M. Moore's Company, Co. F (Sumter Shorter Guards), 4th Regiment Militia, was photographed during the Spring of 1862 wearing a uniform of this pattern, which consisted of a seven-button grey wool jacket with dark standing collar, shoulder straps and pointed cuffs. His pants were plain grey without seam stripes.

Other styles of uniform were also issued at this time. Whilst encamped near Centreville, Virginia, during November 1861, the 12th Alabama Infantry received 'grey dress uniforms' which consisted of 'scissor tailed coats' and caps that 'fell over in front with a place for letters.' Similarly, members of the

Cherokee Rangers, Co. I, 19th Alabama Infantry, were photographed wearing plain grey eight-button wool and cotton coats with swallow tails; and grey pants. By 22 January 1862, Alabama had spent $375,000 supplying their troops in Virginia with uniforms. This clothing was distributed via a state depot situated at Richmond.

Brothers in the Billy Gilmer Grays, Co. F, 14th Alabama Infantry, raised at Hickory Flat on 31 July 1861 by Captain M.P. Ferrell. This unit added extensive trim and unusual external pockets to their version of the uniform adopted by the state in August 1861. Corporal Jefferson Strickland (left) has taken his small brass-framed pistol from its leather holster and placed it in his pocket. Sergeant Madison Strickland (right) has a Colt Navy Revolver pushed in his waist belt, a smaller calibre revolver in his pocket, and a sheathed bowie knife on his right hip. Both men hold Enfield rifled muskets. Margaret P. Milford via VSAMHI/ photo by Jim Enos.

Georgia

The enrolled militia system of Georgia possessed little tangible reality during the decade before the civil war. Nonetheless, on paper it consisted of 13 divisions, each with two brigades. Each brigade embraced from two to 12 counties, dependent on the population. The Volunteer Militia, on the other hand, was thriving if ill-controlled, particularly after John Brown's raid in 1859. By February 1861 there were 173 companies on the rolls, with some 35 more in the process of organisation. In that year, the adjutant general sent out Special Order No. 24 to all volunteer militia companies instructing them to report on their arms, equipment and uniform. The collective response shows units in swallow-tail coatees, frock coats and jackets, with shakoes, forage caps, slouch hats and kepis, in all styles and colours. Many had an undress, aswell as full dress, uniform. Although Georgia seceded from the Union on 19 January 1861, preparations for secession, and for raising a state military force, began in early November 1860.

The Sumter Light Guards became Company K, 4th Georgia Infantry. In this image, probably taken by Tucker and Perkins, of Broad Street, Augusta, during March 1861, they parade in their dark blue jackets, pants, and caps, trimmed with buff. Their First National flag is held high by the color sergeant, with color guard either side. Georgia Department of Archives and History.

Governor Joseph E. Brown urged the legislature to raise a million dollars, and accept 10,000 troops, for state defense. The office of adjutant general was revived, and the volunteer companies collectively offered their services to the state. Consequently, Fort Pulaski, near Savannah, was occupied by the 1st Regiment Georgia Volunteers, a volunteer militia unit commanded by Colonel Alexander R. Lawton, on 3 January 1861. The Augusta Independent Volunteer Battalion seized the Augusta Arsenal twenty days later. The companies involved in these actions wore a variety of distinctive fatigue uniforms. The Republican Blues, Co. C, 1st Regiment, wore dark blue shell jackets trimmed wih white cord on collar, shoulder straps and pointed cuffs; sky blue pants with broad white seam stripes; and dark blue forage caps. The Irish Volunteers, Co. E, wore 'service hats, jackets, dark pantaloons and waist belts.' Within the Augusta Battalion, the Clinch Rifles donned their 'dark green cloth' shell jackets, possibly with yellow lace trim around collar and on cuffs; black pants, and green Model 1856 caps with stiffening removed. The Richmond Hussars wore an army blue shirt trimmed with yellow, a black Hardee hat with black feather plumes, and sky blue pants with broad seam stripes.

It was not until 15 February 1861 that Adjutant

These members of the Clinch Rifles, Co. A, 5th Georgia, were photographed in camp at Macon on 10 May 1861, the day before they were mustered in. Generally relaxing in civilian clothing, several wear their dark green uniform caps and trousers. Note the company initials painted on tent and camp equipage, and their stacked Model 1841 Rifles and sword bayonets. USAMHI/photo by Jim Enos.

General Henry C. Wayne prescribed state uniform regulations via General Orders No. 4 which referred solely to the two infantry regiments and two battalions of artillery and cavalry which made up the Georgia Army, organised that month. Accordingly, officers were to wear frock coat and trouser of dark blue cloth, the latter 'to be made loose, and to spread well over the foot.' For full dress, general and staff officers wore the U.S. Army dress (Hardee) hat, looped up on the right side with a large gilt Georgia state seal button, with gold cord and three black ostrich feathers. A *chapeau bras*, or cocked hat, could also be worn if preferred. Captains and other subordinate officers wore the same, with two black feathers, and the regimental number embroidered in one inch-high numerals on a black velvet ground. Officers were also permitted to wear a blue chasseur cap for fatigue. Commissioned rank was indicated by either epaulettes

The uniform worn by Private James Greer of the West Point Guards, Co. D, 4th Georgia Infantry, was described thus by the *Augusta Daily Constitutional and Sentinel* on May 1861 - 'Their suit is gray, of Roswell manufacture, black stripe on pants, gray cloth caps'. Alabama State Archives.

M. H. Cutter enlisted in the Floyd Rifles, Co. C, 2nd Battalion, Georgia Infantry on 20 April 1861. He wears a double-breasted black frock coat. David Wynn Vaughan collection.

or shoulder straps.

Non-commissioned officers and enlisted mens' frock coats and pants were of 'Georgia Cadet gray', with black 'cord or welt' trim on collar and pointed cuffs for infantry, and orange for artillery. The cavalry battalion probably wore a grey jacket. Headgear consisted of the Hardee hat looped up on the left, without feather, and with a worsted gold cord and gilt company letter in front. A blue flannel sack coat was prescribed for fatigue. Non-commissioned officers' chevrons corresponded to those of the U.S. Army.

Although this uniform was meant only to apply to the small Georgia Army, the same clothing was furnished to the 1st Regiment Georgia Regulars, a three-year infantry unit, on 17 July 1861. Furthermore, according to contemporary newspaper reports during 1861, many infantry companies either adopted or changed to grey uniforms trimmed with black, whilst most officers wore blue. A typical account is held within the memoirs of Captain James C. Nesbet who

commanded the Silver Grays, Co. H, 21st Georgia Infantry: 'The uniforms of gray, made to order, had to be shipped by E. Winship, Macon, Georgia, for which I paid.... The men, uniformed in gray, presented a good appearance. The lieutenants were uniformed in home-made blue jeans. My uniform was of regular U.S. Army blue, tailor-made, a present (with my sword and belt) from my sister...'

To assist in uniforming its state forces, the Georgia legislature appropriated $648,780, which was used to pay local manufacturers, plus Northern military suppliers in New York and Philadelphia, from whom Georgia agents had actively purchased goods up to April 1861. On the 10th of that month, Governor Brown requisitioned his state for 3,000 military companies, and required them all to have a plain service uniform and 'change of underclothing.' After numerous enquiries regarding the type of service uniform needed, he announced on 28 May that the volunteers should have a coat or jacket; two pairs of trousers; one forage or fatigue cap; two flannel shirts, preferably grey or blue (not red as they presented 'an

Private William Favor of the Franklin Volunteers, Co. G, 7th Georgia Infantry, appears to be wearing his 'Sicilian' cap over the crown of his hat! Several stars are just visible on the dark area of cloth. USAMHI/photo by Jim Enos.

excellent mark for the enemy'); and one light, black necktie. In response, a wide variety of uniforms were adopted. Those reported being worn by companies passing through Augusta by the *Daily Chronicle and Sentinel* during this period are quite typical, e.g. Burke Guards (Co. A, 3rd Georgia) - 'Their uniform is dark gray, trimmed with green; officers with coats, privates with jackets, slouched hats'; Brown Rifles (Co. B, 3rd Georgia) - 'gray, with red trimmings'; Dawson Grays (Co. C, 3rd Georgia) - 'Georgia gray, trimmed with black'; Home Guard (Co. D, 3rd Georgia) - 'Georgia gray': Governor's Guards (Co. E, 3rd Georgia) - 'a red jacket, blue-black pants, with white stripe, and German fatigue cap': Wilkinson Rifles (Co. F, 3rd Georgia) - 'Georgia kersey, buff-colored': Southern Rifles (Co. A, 4th Georgia) - 'Georgia gray, trimmed with black velvet': LeGrange Light Guard (Co. B, 4th Georgia) - '"Roswell gray" jackets and pants trimmed with black. Georgia buttons': Twiggs Volunteers (Co. C, 4th Georgia) - 'a durable cassimere, manufactured at the Eagle Factory, Columbus; the pants with black

Unidentified soldier, probably a Georgian, wearing a very elaborate 'Sicilian' stocking cap, tinted red, along with his waist sash, in the original image. David Wynn Vaughan collection.

stripe. A portion of the company wear red shirts with both cloth and glazed caps': Baldwin Blues (Co. H, 4th Georgia) - 'a dark blue; very neat and serviceable'.

The 'flannel shirts' worn also varied greatly, prompting Governor Brown's instructions. A letter from 'Camp Oglethorpe', near Macon, dated 5 April 1861, describes troops wearing: 'red shirts, blue shirts,

Orderly Sergeant Marmaduke H. Marshall of the Webster Confederate Guards, Co. K, 17th Georgia Infantry, wears a version of the distinctive Georgia-pattern jacket with black three-pointed sleeve patches as issued by the state during the Fall of 1861. Note the unusual lozenge and single chevron on one sleeve only. His sword belt plate curiously bears the Palmetto Tree device associated with South Carolina. He holds an elaborate militia officer's sword, which suggests that this image was taken shortly after his promotion to 2nd Lieutanant in August 1862. Georgia Department of Archives and History.

gray shirts, and shirts without order and indescribable to an unpractised eye...' Those worn by the Clinch Rifles encamped at the same place the following month included polka-dots and patterned bib fronts.

The zouave fashion was represented in Georgia by a boys' company commanded by Captain Speillers called the Young Zouaves, formed in Augusta in 1860, who wore 'bright blue jackets and fiery red trousers.' About thirty members of the Macon Volunteers, led by Captain R. A. Smith, wore a version of the zouave uniform. The Macon *Telegraph* reported: 'a group of gentlemen surrounding a figure, who, from his fantastic dress... was either a Japanese, a Chinese, a Sioux Indian, or one of the latest importation from Africa. We drew near, and discovered the fanastic

figure to be that of our fellow-citizen, Mr. D. B. W., Orderly of the Volunteers, and was dressed in the uniform of the Macon Volunteer Zouaves. This uniform is made of bright cloth, and in a strange fashion, and presents a picturesque and graceful appearance.'

The 'Sicilian'-style stocking cap, complete with tassels and havelock, was also popular amongst Georgia troops early in the war. The Thompson Guards, Co. F, 10th Georgia Infantry, wore 'cap covers... parti-colored, or plaid, long and pointed, and so arranged that they may be thrown back on the neck or over the visor.' Other companies photographed wearing this item include the Gardner Volunteers, Co. H, and the Henry Volunteers, Co. K, of the 22nd Georgia Infantry. It was fashionable to wear these caps either over, or under, slouch hats and forage caps.

Numerous small firms throughout the state were involved in clothing the growing number of Georgia units in 1861. Henry Lathrop and Co. in Savannah employed 75 women to make uniforms of different kinds. The Bellville Factory of Augusta, owned by George Schley, produced 'a handsome and durable assortment of solid colored and striped twilled cotton goods for soldiers' wear.' By June 1861, they had furnished several companies with serviceable uniforms – among them the Indendent Blues, who became Co. D, 10th Georgia Infantry. Other important suppliers included the Eagle Factory at Columbus, the Milledgeville Manufacturing Co., and the Ivy Woollen Mill at Roswell. The latter, established by Connecticut Yankee Roswell King in 1839, produced cloth of a dark bluish-grey cast called 'Roswell gray'. These efforts were supplemented by the numerous aid societies established in every county in the state. Typical of these was the Ladies Aid Society of Clarke County which bought cloth with money raised by taxes, issuing bonds, or soliciting subscriptions. Local tailors measured and cut out the uniforms, which were sewn together by the ladies of the Society and friends. Some counties, like Clarke, continued to supply their menfolk throughout the entire conflict.

During the autumn of 1861, Governor Brown began to realise that Georgia troops in Virginia would not be adequately clothed for the oncoming winter. Therefore, on 4 September he placed advertisements in state newspapers expressing a need to purchase enough woollen cloth for 30,000 suits of clothing, plus 30,000 pairs of shoes. The success of this appeal may be gauged by a letter from Brown to the new Confederate Secretary of War, Judah P. Benjamin, dated 19 October, inquiring whether clothing for troops in government service had to be uniform, or whether it

The Pittman brothers, John (centre), Jesse (left), and Thomas (right) enlisted in the Quitman Greys, Co. I, 11th Georgia Infantry during July 1861. Georgia Department of Archives and History.

Captain Dilmus L. Jarrett commanded the Jackson County Volunteers, Co. C, 18th Georgia Infantry, in June 1861. He holds a militia officer's sword. Rank is indicated by Federal-style shoulder straps. Note the single button sewn on the point of his cuff facings. USAMH/photo by Jim Enos.

could be 'any substantial woolen clothing.'

A number of photographs of Georgia infantrymen taken during this period indicate that grey shell jackets of remarkably similar styles were being issued. All were distinguished by black three-pointed sleeve patches with small buttons, set well in from the cuff edge. One version, worn by members of the West Point Guards, Co. D, 4th Georgia Infantry, and the Franklin Volunteers, Co. G, 7th Georgia Infantry, is fastened by six buttons, with solid black collar and shoulder straps, and pockets on each breast, about level with the third button from the top. A private in the Roswell Guards, Co. H, 7th Georgia, donned a slightly different version fastened by eight buttons, with a black tab or loop with small button attached to a grey collar. Yet another eight-button version with collar edged with black tape was worn by a member of the Ben Hill Volunteers, Co. F, 21st Georgia Infantry. This similarity in jacket design possibly indicates that a standard pattern was being made available to Soldier Aid Societies until at least March 1862. The trousers

accompanying these jackets generally seem to be plain, whilst headgear mainly seems to have consisted of black, drab or grey slouch hats.

As the result of a call for twelve additional regiments in February 1862, the Confederate government agreed to furnish all clothing and equipment. By the

Privates Daniel, John and Pleasant Chitwood enlisted in the Bartow County Yankee Killers, Co. A, 23rd Georgia Infantry. They all wear 'Checked Cottonade' shirts popular as fatigue wear with many Southern companies. They hold large Bowie knifes of identical manufacture, and Colt Model 1849 Pocket Revolvers. Georgia Department of Archives and History.

fall of that year the supply system had broken down, and Governor Brown reported to the legislature on 6 November that 'Georgia troops in Confederate service are almost destitute of clothes and shoes, and must suffer terribly this winter...' This led to the passage of 'An Act to appropriate money to procure and furnish clothing, shoes, caps or hats, and blankets for the soldiers from Georgia...,' and the establishment of a state clothing bureau at Augusta under the supervision of Captain George W. Evans, and a shoe manufactory run by Captain E.M. Field at Marietta. Based on the appropriation of $1,500,00, Quartermaster General Ira R. Foster was able to report on 25 March 1863 that the following had been supplied to Georgia troops in nineteen regiments and 2 battalions in Confederate service in Virginia, Tennessee, and South Carolina: 4,556 coats, 5,288 pants, 4,646 hats, 5,449 shirts and 5,744 shoes. These articles were mostly shipped to their destination in the charge of bonded State Agents.

In a few cases, the Quartermasters of Regiments had personally collected them from the storehouses. At that time, Foster stated that manufactured clothing still on hand amounted to 7,272 coats, 9,257 pants, 129 hats, 10,400 shirts and 5,878 shoes. Also available was 12,983 yards of osnaburgs, 18,850 yards of shirting, 6,410 yards of kerseys, 970 yards of duck, and 35,063 pounds of leather. Despite the latter, he warned that Georgia troops would 'suffer more the coming winter than they did the past...' unless further appropriations were made whilst materials were still available. Consequently, on 26 April 1863 Governor Brown directed that a further $2,000,000 should be expended on the purchase and manufacture of clothes and shoes.

By November 1863, Foster was able to report that his bureau had issued hats, clothing and shoes to 44 regiments, seven battalions, and two companies, as follows: '4,719 hats, 7,291 jackets, 8,828 pants, 9,185 shirts, 8,036 drawers, 12,294 shoes, 7,517 socks.' He also had on hand nearly: 'forty thousand suits of clothes, which are ready for distribution among the troops as their necessities may require.'

Despite increasing problems with shortage of supply and difficulties with labour, especially after the fall of Atlanta, Quartermaster General Foster main-

tained a supply of clothing to Georgia troops during 1864. A considerable amount of the uniform cloth, and other goods, continued to be run through the blockade, whilst raw wool was acquired in Texas in exchange for 'colored osnaburg'. During the closing months of the war, sufficient clothing remained on hand to ensure that Georgia's contingent in the Confederate army, which totalled between 25,000 and 30,000 men, remained well clad whilst access remained to supply routes.

Three soldiers in examples of frock coats supplied between 1862-63. Private James Anderson Scruggs, Gibson Volunteers, Co. A, (left); and Private Thomas C. Mobley, Burke Volunteers, Co. D, 48th Georgia Infantry (centre), wear coats of possible South Carolina provenance, as their regiment was stationed at Camp Donaldson, near Grahamville, from 4 March until 1 May 1862. Private William Henry Witcher (right) enlisted in the 3rd Battalion, Georgia Sharpshooters, organised on 8 June 1863. His coat may well have been one of the 7,272 coats the Georgia Quartermaster Department had 'on hand' in March 1863. USAMHI/photo by Jim Enos; Woodruff Library, Emory University; USAMHI/photo by Jim Enos.

Louisiana

The only regulations governing the uniform of the Louisiana military prior to 1861 were those of 12 January 1857 which applied purely to the Commanding General and staff. This was based on U.S. regulation dress except for state buttons. Therefore, when the 'Pelican state' seceded from the Union on 26 January 1861 the volunteers who rushed to her standard were uniformed in a multitude of different uniforms which illustrated its large foreign-born population. Military dress ranged in style from French, Irish, Italian, Scottish, and German, to those of the many 'native' American companies of light infantry and riflemen. Several battalion militia uniforms did see some early war service. The Washington Artillery of New Orleans, nicknamed 'The Game Cocks' by President Jefferson Davis, joined Confederate forces in Virginia in June 1861 wearing a uniform made by the leading tailors of the city. This consisted of a dark blue frock coat with red collar and pointed cuffs, white shoulder and waist belts, and sky blue pants with red seam stripes. A red kepi with blue band and yellow lace, adopted late in 1860, replaced their pre-war Model 1851 dress cap. White canvas gaiters were worn for infantry service. During First Manassas they also placed red flannel stripes on their left arms above the elbow to avoid being mistaken for the enemy, despite General (P.) G.T. Beauregard's orders that all 'wing badges' should be removed on the eve of battle. Later in 1861, this battalion sent their frock coats to Richmond for use on furlough, and adopted a blue-grey shell jacket with red piping on cuffs and shoulder straps, with blue jean pants, and red cap with blue band. The 5th Company, Washington Artllery, organized as a reserve on 27 May 1861, wore a similar uniform except that their shell jackets were dark blue trimmed red on collar and shoulder straps.

The Orleans Battalion of Artillery, which first became involved in the seizure of forts Jackson and St. Philip below New Orleans, and later converted to infantry, wore a plain blue jacket and pants of grey-blue Kentucky jean tucked into black leather gaiters, and a blue kepi trimmed with red. The first uniform chosen by the Chasseurs a Pied, or Louisiana Foot Rifles, was described by the New Orleans *Daily Crescent* as being 'finer and much neater fitting than that of the famed French soldiers... Their very small caps, perched on top of their heads; their tight fitting, dark colored, short tailed coats, with their slender red fringes and green epaulettes; their enormous mouse colored breeches, falling in loose folds below their knees, their tight yellow leggins and their white gaiters - all these new things in military dress in this country, combined to give this new company a very novel and picturesque appearance.' By early 1861 this battalion had adopted a blue undress uniform with white gaiters.

The Orleans Guard Battalion, which was designated the 13th Louisiana Battalion, wore a dark blue frock coat and pants, and red forage cap for full dress. By February 1861 they had a fatigue uniform composed of 'dark blue kepis... jackets or short coats and pants of the same color, all trimmed with red, black belts and cartouche boxes.' During the battle of Corinth on 3-4 October 1862, the 6th Kentucky, at the sight of this 'blue uniform brought out from New Orleans', mistook the Orleans Guard Battalion for the enemy and fired on them, killing two men! Shortly thereafter, they were ordered to 'turn their uniform wrong side outwards, thus giving them the appearance of going to a masquerade ball.'

The Legion Française, formed among the French citizens of New Orleans, adopted a copy of the French infantry dress which consisted of a horizon-blue coat, and red pants and cap. The Confederate Guards Response Battalion paraded in 'gray frock coats, caps and white pants.' The Garibaldi Legion, expanded from a volunteer militia company called the Garibaldi Guards, wore a 'black cocked hat, with a black plume on the cocked side, the stem of the plume... being covered with little feathers of red, green and white, (the colors of Italy) and the whole secured with a pelican button. A red jacket, tight fitting to the waist but spreading out at the hips; a black belt around the waist, with cartouche-box behind, and the jacket buttoned up to the chin with Pelican buttons. Grey trousers, of the largest Zouave style, bulging out as low on the knee; and then buff leather leggins, strapped and buckled the rest of the way down to the gaiters.'

Regarding some of the individual companies of Louisiana volunteer militia in 1861, the Orleans Flying Artillery, commanded by Captain Everitt, formerly of the Bengal cavalry, chose: 'a black navy cap with gold band and seven white stars around, glazed top painted white, and gold chain chin strap; a scarlet flannel or cassimere jacket with epaulettes, navy blue pantaloons, with patent leather bottoms and straps of chain; heavy boots with boxed spurs, a black sword belt, long swords, and shoulder cross belts for cartridge box, with a brace of large navy revolvers.'

The British Guard under Captain Shannon wore a suit of 'white flannel with blue and silver facings.' The Belgian Guards' uniform was composed of 'dark green frock coats, trimmed with yellow, and pants and cap of same.' That worn by the Orleans Rifles was in imitation of '... the Kentucky or frontier Riflemen, consisting of broad brimmed black hats cocked on one side, loose hunting shirts of green with black fringes; pants yellow to the knee and below that black in imitation of yellow buckskin and leggins; and small cartouche boxes slung at the side.'

The Louisiana Guerrillas wore 'a velvet hunting jacket, *mi tasses*, or leggins, similar to those worn by Indians, cotton pantaloons and an otter skin cap.'

During the weeks prior to secession, Louisiana began to recruit companies for two 'Regular' regiments, one each of infantry and artillery. After an unsuccessful attempt to contract for cloth for uniforms for these units, a solution was found in having it made at the State Penitentiary at Baton Rouge, where a textile factory had existed since at least 1857. According to a report in the *Charleston Daily Courier*, this institution possessed '5632 spindles, 200 looms, and the necessary carding machines, with the capacity to consume about fifteen bales of cotton, and turn out twelve thousand yards of cloth a day.' The full dress regimental uniform received by the 1st Regular Infantry was to be based on 'the rules and regulations of the U.S. Army', and consisted of a dark blue frock coat and pants, and blue cap. It is doubtful whether this was ever received by the whole unit. A company of regulars involved in the occupation of the New

William H. Martin (left) of the 7th Louisiana Infantry wears an example of the uniform issued by the state during the Fall of 1861. His father, James Martin (right), wears the full dress uniform of the Continental Guard, Louisiana Militia, which consisted of a blue cut-away coat faced with buff, buff breeches, and black tricorne hat with red and white feathers. Confederate Memorial Hall.

Orleans barracks during January 1861 wore an undress uniform, issued around the 13th of that month, which consisted of 'a dark blue jacket, coming down to the hip, single-breasted, with five pelican buttons, and dark blue pants, with a stripe of yellow cord.' As yet without headgear, they presented a 'motley array of silk hats, slouched tiles and glazed caps' when drawn up for inspection. According to the *Daily Delta*, they were soon to receive 'a graceful looking Zouave cap, of navy blue cloth.' On 14 January, Company B of this regiment, originally commanded by Captain John A. Jacques, 'adopted a neat gray undress cap with pelican buttons obtained at D'Arcy's Store, the stock of which was disposed of in an hour.'

Regarding uniforms for the Louisiana volunteer regiments and battalions raised for Confederate service, the organization of which began on 25 April 1861, individual companies began their war experience

The Tiger Rifles, Co. B, 1st Special Battalion. The zouave uniform received by this unit consisted of a light-weight mazarine blue jacket with deep red wool trim, full zouave trousers, or *serouel*, made from blue and white 'Hamilton' mattress ticking, deep red woollen shirts with placket front fastened by small porcelain buttons, red zouave cap with 'tassel down the back', and white gaiters over 'colored stockings'. From descriptions and artefacts by Ron Field.

wearing either what they could provide themselves, or what local aid associations could come up with. The 1st Louisiana Infantry Battalion, commanded by Colonel Charles D. Dreux, arrived at Pensacola in a variety of garb. The Louisiana Guard, Co. A, wore a 'blue roundabout', or shell jacket, trimmed with buff, 'French army pattern' dark blue caps trimmed with gilt braid, and white gaiters. The Crescent City Rifles, Co. B, paraded in a suit of 'light gray, Zouave style, with golden crescents embroidered on their kepis,' plus 'newly washed [white] gaiters.'

The Orleans Cadets, Co. F, was the first Louisiana company mustered into Confederate service. Their full dress consisted of a nine-button dark grey frock with solid black trim on the collar, shoulder straps and pointed cuffs; grey chasseur-pattern forage caps with a black band and quartered with thin black piping; black

waist belts and grey pants with black seam stripes. For 'camp or fatigue' they arrived on the coast wearing a uniform put together in New Orleans from 'gray tweeds made in Georgia,' composed of a seven-button zouave-style jacket trimmed all around, and on cuffs, with black edging and braid respectively. Their very full-cut pants were also trimmed with narrow black seam stripes.

Enroute through Montgomery, Alabama, members of this battalion were presented with a version of the ubiquitous 'Sicilian' cap of 'sugar loaf shape and of the tri-color red, white and blue, which make the wearers in appearance quite "a la Zouave".'

The 1st Special Battalion, or 2nd Louisiana Infantry Battalion, raised by Chatham Roberdeau Wheat, who had seen military service in Mexico, Cuba, Nicaragua, and Italy, was composed of a mixture of 'Irish roustabouts and riff-raff' of New Orleans, filibusters, and the sons of wealthy planters. Some members of this unit had taken part in the Lopez expedition and, until they acquired uniforms, still wore their 'off-white drill pants or breeches with gaiters or boots, red flannel shirt, and broad-brimmed hat..'. The Tiger Rifles, Co. B, initially decorated their hats with 'pictures of tigers in attitudes and slogans.' Their zouave uniform was paid for by A. Keene

Richards, a wealthy citizen of New Orleans.

Other Louisiana units initially wearing zouave uniform included Coppens' Louisiana Zouaves, or the 1st Confederate States Zouave Battalion; the 2nd Zouave Battalion, commanded by Major St. Leon Dupeire; and the Avegno Zouaves, also known as the Battalion of Governor's Guards. This six-company battalion from New Orleans, commanded by Major Anatole Avegno, wore blue jackets and full red trousers. By 11 September 1861, they formed part of the 13th Louisiana Infantry. John W. Labouisse, an officer in the Southern Celts, Co. A of the same regiment, was photographed early in the war wearing a grey jacket and trousers which also had a zouave appearance. His jacket was fastened by 11 small ball-buttons, with light-coloured trim on pointed cuffs. The rank of first lieutenant was indicated by two bars sewn on the turned down collar. His full-cut pants had dark-coloured seam stripes.

A number of individual Louisiana volunteer, militia, and cadet companies are believed to have worn full or partial zouave dress. The Hope Guard paraded in 'Zouave jackets and pants of dark blue, neatly trimmed, white belts, and blue kepis....' The Young Cadets, also called the Louisiana Cadets, attached to the Orleans Rifle Battalion, wore a 'neat and elegant Zouave uniform of light blue,' with black caps. The Home Sentinels, a militia company of Iberville Parish which did not enlist into Confederate service, 'wore a Zouave-like uniform with close-fitting jacket and red-striped pants.' In Monroe, a small North Louisiana town, two boys' companies - the Monroe Zouaves and the Monroe Cadets - combined to form the Ouachita Fencibles, and were furnished 'colorful uniforms and armed with double-barrelled shotguns.' Another company from New Orleans, called the Monroe Guards, which later became Co. K, 5th Louisiana, had a vivandiere called Leona Neville who wore a 'nicely-fitting black alpaca uniform.'

Regarding artillery, the Watson Artillery, originally commanded by Captain Allen A. Bursley, wore a steel grey shell jacket, pants and kepi trimmed with crimson facings. After travelling up the Mississippi River via Memphis to report for duty at Columbus, Kentucky, the unit became so dissatisfied with its officers that they 'removed the "W.A." from their caps.' The Donaldsonville Artillery, a volunteer militia company founded in 1837, had a dress uniform similar to that of the Orleans Guard Battalion, but in 1861 adopted a fatigue outfit consisting of a grey shell jacket, with shoulder straps, fastened by nine gilt buttons bearing a flaming bomb over crossed cannon, with the inscription 'Les Canonniers de Donaldsonville.' Pants were plain grey. Caps were also grey with dark, possibly red band, with gilt crossed-cannon insignia in front.

State clothing provision for Louisiana troops came later in the year, with over $600,000 being spent on the task for approximately 20 units. Typical was that received by the 3rd Louisiana Infantry in Missouri during September. Each man was given 'one red flannel shirt, one cotton shirt, one plaid linsey shirt, to be worn over the cotton shirt, one pair plaid linsey or flannel drawers, one pair of heavy woolen jeans pants and a long jacket, lined inside with linsey, and padded on the shoulders to carry the gun with ease.' This was elsewhere described as being 'of substantial material known as jeans, being grayish-blue in color, with the exception of Company K [Pelican Rifles], which is of dark brown.' The cloth for this issuance were also produced at the State Penitentiary, being subseqently made up by the Ladies of Baton Rouge. Uniforms sent to the 1st and 2nd regiments were lost, or delayed. The 4th and 5th regiments also received theirs during September. On 19 August 1861, Lieutenant-Colonel Charles de Choiseul wrote: 'I am getting made new fatigue uniforms, for the entire command, of a light blue heavy cloth, a very pretty and serviceable uniform indeed.' A member of the same regiment wrote on 1 October 1861: 'the new uniform is now all here complete, and I can assure you to see 1000 men all dressed alike makes for a different impression on a spectator than a variety of colours, caps, and hats, coats and jackets, and such like mixtures.'

The whole of General Richard Taylor's Louisiana brigade, composed of the 6th, 7th, 8th and 9th Louisiana regiments, plus Wheat's 1st Special Battalion, were reviewed in this uniform, with white gaiters, during May 1862. That received by the 8th Louisiana revealed the problems the State Penitentiary workshops experienced producing cloth of standard quality and colour. Some of the clothing was in appearance as 'absurd as a harlequin dress, the body and sleeves being of diverse colors and materials.'

Excluded from state issuance were the 14th Louisiana, and the 3rd Infantry Battalion. By December 1861, the former were reported to have 'received no clothing of any description from the state... they are not in a situation to purchase clothing other than that furnished by their officers from the $25 allowed by the Government for six months clothing.' By 9 March 1862, the 21st Louisiana were 'airing the new clothing so opportunely sent by the Governor of Louisiana.' The uniforms of the 24th Louisiana, 'consisting of strong, substantial gray cloth, and very neatly and handsomely made[,] were furnished in 3 days...' during the same month. *(continued on p.56)*

Private David E. Lusby, Issaquena Artillery Mississippi volunteers. David Wynn Vaughan collection.

Private James M. Stedham, Company A, 25th Alabama Infantry, wears an unusual dark grey, woollen shell jacket with shoulder straps, possibly of the type issued by his state after August 1861. David Wynnn Vaughan collection.

Coppens' Louisiana Zouaves, or 1st Confederate States Zouave Battalion, at Pensacola in 1861.

New Orleans resident George Auguste Gaston Coppens raised a battalion of Zouaves in March 1861. The unit was made up of men from virtually all European nations, many of whom had previous military experience. Organisation, drill, orders and dress were modelled on that of the French Zouaves. The unit saw service at Pensacola in Florida, and in the campaigns of Northern Virginia, Maryland and North Carolina.

The original uniform worn by N.C.O.s and enlisted men (left) consisted of a close-fitting soft red flannel skull cap, or *calotte,* worn on the back of the head with a deep blue tassel hanging down at the back; a dark blue close fitting collarless flannel vest trimmed with red around the collar and down the middle of the chest; a loose flannel jacket similar in cut to the original 1830 Zouave jacket, missing the characteristic 'tombeau', or false pocket, but trimmed with red around the cuff and jacket edges; a broad sky blue merino wool waist sash; bright red full baggy trousers, or *serouels;* and white hemp gaiters, over which were worn black 'gutta percha' leggings, or *jambieres.*

Vivandieres, ladies armed with barrels of brandy who

brought succour to the men and nursed the wounded (centre) were quite common in the earliest volunteer units, both North and South. Those in Coppens' command wore a version of the Battalion uniform, described as consisting of 'a pair of high heel shoes, over the top of which shine white gaiter tops; above these are tight fitting pieces of leather extending to the knee; there they unite with red, wide drawers; they have a blue skirt with red border from waist to their knee and a blue jacket from waist to neck.'

Officers' dress (right) conformed in many ways to that of the French Zouaves. Their kepi appears to have had a red crown, sky blue band and gold lace quartering and quatrefoil, the number of these lace strips indicating rank similar to the Confederate and French Zouave systems. The frock coat was very dark blue (almost black) single-breasted, closely tailored to the torso, very full skirt to below mid-thigh, low collar with round edge, and rank being indicated by gold lace in Hungarian knots that reached almost to the shoulder. The colour of their full cut trousers is conjectural. Painting by Richard Hook.

As cloth grew scarce these long jackets, or coats, were quickly replaced by shell jackets fastened by a variation of six, eight or nine-buttons, usually trimmed around the edges, collar, shoulder straps, and cuffs, with half-inch wide black braid. Many volunteers received chasseur-style caps, often quartered with thin black piping and bands of various colours, suggesting that some regimental preference may have existed.

Members of the Confederate States Rangers, Co. K, 10th Louisiana were photographed wearing slouch hats looped up on the left with their state uniform. Trousers were full cut with black seam stripes. The cap style generally worn with this series of issuance may also have been influenced by that of the prestigious Orleans Cadets described above. Likewise, the jackets seem to follow the pattern adopted for fatigue by that company at the beginning of 1861. Alternatively, the choice of the latter may have been dictated by the economics of war.

The full dress of the Orleans Cadets described

Second Lieutenant James C. Wilson, of the Bienville Blues, Co. C, 5th Louisiana Infantry, wore this dark blue frock and lighter-coloured braided cap when he mustered into Confederate service on 4 June 1861. He holds what appears to be a Virginia Manufactory artillery sabre with an iron guard.
Confederate Memorial Hall, New Orleans, Louisiana.

above may have influenced the pattern of uniform acquired by a number of Louisiana units after receipt of their state issue. Paul Thibodaux, a member of the Lafourche Creoles, Co. G, 18th Louisiana, was photographed after promotion to corporal on 17 December 1861, and before receiving a wound at Shiloh on 6-7 April 1862, wearing a uniform virtually identical to that of the Orleans Cadets. Other photographic examples include that of Private William Y. Dixon of the Hunter Rifles, Co. G, 4th Louisiana, taken on 7 March 1862. Fastened by only five buttons, Dixon's coat has a turned-down black collar, and a small button at the point of his solid black-faced cuffs. Private Edwin F. Jennison, Claiborne Guards, Co. F, 2nd Louisiana, was photographed sometime before his death at Malvern Hill on 1 July 1862 in similar garb. Private William Strong, 2nd Louisiana Cavalry, wore what appears to have been a cavalry version of this uniform, with yellow-faced collar, cuffs and shoulder straps

This 'Orleans Cadet'-style frock coat may have been issued to Louisiana troops even later in the war. Whilst in winter quarters at Camp Qui Vive at Fausse Point, Louisiana, during the period November 1862 to April 1863, the 18th Louisiana were 'furnished with a lot of Confederate gray cloth [probably still being manufactured at the State Penitentiary for the Confederate States quartermaster department], which was distributed among the different camps.' The regimental quartermaster, Major Silas T. Grisamore, recalled: 'Col. [Leopold L.] Armant ordered me to go to St. Martinsville to a tailor.' There follows a long, humorous description of the uniforms, which were almost all cut too small, including: '... [we] pulled the garment so high up behind the neck that the buttons [on the coat tails] were right between the shoulders.' The buttons were 'real shining brass beauties', whilst the 'wrist bands', or cuffs, on the coat were described as being 'trimmed with black...'.

Opposite
Private Thomas Taylor, Phoenix Company, 8th Louisiana Infantry, wears an example of the uniform issued by the state during the Fall of 1861, and holds a M1842 Musket. His accoutrements include an Enfield Rifle Musket cartridge box and a U.S. regulation cap pouch. Eleanor S. Brockenbrough Library, The Museum of the Confederacy, Richmond, Virginia.

Texas

On the eve of the Civil War, the militia of Texas consisted of five divisions, with regiments raised on a county-wide basis. As in most other states, the enrolled militia was virtually dormant. Uniformed volunteer militia companies were attached to each battalion and regiment, but only seven of these existed in 1858: the Alamo Rifles of San Antonio; Washington Light Guards, Milam Rifles, and Turner Rifles, of Houston; Galveston Artillery and Lone Star Company, of Galveston; and the Refugio Riflemen. Other units were hastily formed as secession approached, and by 1861 the 1st Regiment Galveston Volunteers was formed which included the Galveston Zouaves, Wigfall Guards and Lone Star Rifles. No state regulations were issued to govern the dress of these companies.

After secession on 1 February 1861 the Committee of Public Safety, appointed by the Secession Convention, elected Ben McCulloch, a Mexican War veteran, colonel of cavalry with orders to raise a force to capture U.S. property, including the arsenal at San Antonio. The force collected by McCulloch included a Volunteer battalion from Gonzales, companies from Lockhart, Sequin and San Antonio; and six companies, or 'castles,' of the Knights of the Golden Circle, a southern rights society founded in 1854. An eye-witness described these units 'appearing, two by two,

on muleback and horseback, mounted and on foot, a motley though quite orderly crowd, carrying the Lone Star flag before them.... Some had coats, but others were in their shirt-sleeves, and not a few were wrapped in old shawls and saddle-blankets.' McCulloch's command was subsequently disbanded when it became apparent that General David E. Twiggs, then commanding the Department of Texas, was not going to offer resistance.

During March 1861, the Committee authorised the organisation of two state cavalry regiments to operate along the northern and southern frontiers. These regiments were mustered into Confederate service for one year, and were designated the 1st (H.E. McCulloch's) and 2nd (J.S. Ford's) Mounted Riflemen. Neither of these units were uniformed, but the former wore red flannel stripes on the shoulders of their civilian shirts and coats, and were armed with Model 1861 Colt revolvers. Companies of non-uniformed citizens called Minute Men were also formed at this time for frontier defense.

Texas received her first call for 8,000 troops from the Confederate Government during April 1861, mainly for coastal defence. This was followed in August by a request for 2,000 troops for service in Virginia. A total of 32 companies were sent to Richmond, where they were organised into the 1st,

The hat of Private Clement Newton Bassett, Co. H, 8th Texas Cavalry, in the Museum of the Confederacy, displays a broken red star with the letter 'R' in the centre, around the whole of which is arranged the letters 'T','E','X','A','S'. Ron Field, from original artefact.

4th, and 5th Infantry Regiments. These, in turn, were formed into the brigade commanded by John Bell Hood.

By the end of 1861, Texas had raised seven regiments and four battalions of infantry, amounting to approximately 7,100 men. About seven companies of artillery were also organised. By contrast, sixteen regiments, three battalions, and three independent companies of cavalry were in the saddle, totalling around 17,338 troopers. These figures illustrate the strong preference of Texans for mounted service, and a natural aversion to foot-slogging! Consequently, a number of cavalry units later had to be dismounted in order to relieve the shortage of infantry.

As with other Confederate states, Texas was burdened with the task of clothing her volunteers. In the absence of a large scale textiles industry, she initially had large stocks of imported cloth and garments which could be turned into uniforms, but there were difficulties making this available. Governor Edward Clark urged companies to come prepared with clothing. Others purchased it on route to war. By September 1861, each county had been made responsible for the acquisition of cloth through private societies, and clothing depots were established in eleven centres. Based on the successful results of this

Surrender of ex-General Twiggs, late of the United States Army, to the Texan Troops in the Gran Plaza, San Antonio, Texas, February 16, 1861. A *Harper's Weekly* **artist depicted the mounted troops present as being uniformly dressed in broad brimmed hats, long duster-style coats, and trousers tucked into boots. An accompanying report generally described this force as being 'plainly dressed, some in Kersey, a fine-looking body of men, with a determined air.'** *Harper's Weekly*, March 23, 1861.

system, the central government requested that Texas continue to clothe her troops and accept the commutation allowance in payment. It was not until late 1862 that Confederate quartermasters took over the task of supplying Texas troops.

Probably the largest source of private supply were the innumerable 'ladies' aid societies.' In Marshall, Texas, four committees were established on 31 July 1861, to collect blankets, hats, socks and shoes for the Lane Rangers, on their way for duty on the Texas frontier. By November, the 'Society' in the vicinity of Lancaster had collected and sent to the 2nd Regiment, Texas Partisan Rangers, commanded by B. Warren Stone, coats, jeans pants, flannel and linsey shirts, boots and shoes. William D. Cater, member of the Lone Star Defenders, Co. C, 3rd Texas Cavalry, recalled that his uniform consisted of: 'Black coats, with vests to match, brown (Huntsville made) jeans pants, black hats and black boots made of calfskin tanned leather. It looked well enough but was very hot to wear in the summer; however, we wore them when ready to start. Nothing was said about the color of the shirt or cravat. Mine...was white and the neckwear was a black silk string tie. This, of course, was soon a thing of the past. Our company started without guns or pistols. I had a knife made in a blacksmith shop with a blade about six inches long, which I carried in a scabbard in the leather belt I added to my uniform.'

The 8th Texas Cavalry, also known as Terry's Texas Rangers, wore a great variety of dress during initial months of service. Enroute east with the first battalion of the regiment, R.C. Hilliard observed of their appearance in a letter home from New Iberia, dated

The Lone Star Rifles, Co. L, 1st Texas Infantry, in front of their quarters at Camp Quantico during the winter of 1861/62. The two men on the left wear the distinctive company fatigue uniform consisting of a plain grey overshirt of a double-breasted fireman's style, with a front 'plastron' fastened by two rows of five buttons. The collar was cut in a broad falling style, while the cuffs, rather than being gathered, appear quite plain, like a jacket, rather than a shirt. PICA03674 Austin History Center, Austin Public Library.

19 September 1861: 'Some in Red, some in Blue - Brow [sic], Greene yellow - some in broad sombreros, some in caps, some without either, as daring a set as ever marched to battle.' After reaching New Orleans, the *Daily Picayune* of 30 September described the Tom Lubbock Rangers, Co. K, as being: '...all athletic men and dress[ed] fantastically in hunting shirts of different materials, with large boots worn on the outside, coming over the knee, with Mexican spurs attached. Some wore fancy Mexican pants trimmed down the side with little brass buttons [conchos], and silk sashes around their waists. Others had the Confederate flag, worked in different colored leathers to represent it, on the legs of their boots.'

Captain John G. Walker, commander of the above company, was further described as wearing a buckskin hunting shirt that hugged his large form, 'immense' boots, large Mexican spurs, sombrero and a 'beautifully worked' Mexican blanket across his shoulders. By late February 1862, the clothing of this company was described as being 'shabby, ragged, and dirty', the only element of uniformity being a red star on their hats and caps. Later in the war, the 8th Texas Cavalry attempted to introduce a hint of uniformity in their clothing by the addition of red trimmings to jackets, shirts and trousers.

Photographic evidence bears further witness to the

great variety of dress worn by Texas mounted units throughout most of the war. Private Wady Williams of the Grimes County Rangers wore a multi-coloured shirt and grey trousers with ball buttons running the length of his leg when he was mustered into the 5th Texas Cavalry on 31 August 1861. The only semblance of military garb worn by Private Japhet Collins of the Bastrop County Rawhides, Co. D, 12th Texas Cavalry, was his Mexican War-style forage cap, and a plain grey woollen overshirt. Private William Burgess, Co. D, 27th Texas Cavalry, volunteered in a homemade uniform coat with solid facing on turned-back front, collar, cuffs and breast pocket top.

Although Texas infantry units were generally clothed in an equally haphazard fashion, those within Hood's Brigade - the only troops from the state to see service in the eastern theatre of the war - were well supplied with uniforms of various cut and style. Within the 1st Texas Infantry, the Star Rifles, Co. D, wore grey jackets and pants, faced in a dark colour on collars, pointed cuffs and trousers stripes. The jackets bore three rows of seven large buttons on the front, linked by a doubled darker cord, with trefoils under the outer buttons, in imitation of military academy dress coats. Headgear consisted of high crowned Hardee hats with brim pinned up on the wearer's left with metal stars. The Reagan Guards, Co. G, wore 'dark suits with bright red stripes.'

Captain Edward Currie of the Crockett Southrons, Co. I, posed for a photograph before he resigned in late December 1861 wearing a grey overshirt with a broad band of black facing colour, edged with light trim down the front opening edge. Two large patch pockets were also edged with half-inch black tape. Shoulder straps and cuffs were also probably faced black. Rank insignia consisted of C.S. regulation bars sewn to the standing collar, the latter being an unusual feature on such a shirt. His light-coloured narrow-brimmed hat was pinned up one side.

According to a memoir written by Private O.T. Hanks, the Texas Invincibles, Co. K, 1st Texas Infantry, left home in uniforms of 'good gray woolen goods cut and fitted by W. A. McClanahan and his helpers, and trimmed with blue collars and cuffs.' The Invincibles' accoutrements were similarly of local manufacture. One member recalled that their 'car-tridge boxes were made of leather by our home saddlers and harness workmen', while another confirmed that he and a local saddler had 'made each of the boys a leather built pistol and knife scabbard and cap box.' These knives, rather than being merely side knives, were intended for use as improvised bayonets, and were made by local blacksmiths from

The most unusual dress in Texas mounted service must have been that of Captain Samuel J. Richardson, who commanded an independent company of cavalry. Although his wide-brimmed black slouch hat and plain shirt may be considered normal wear, his jaguar-skin trousers, with conchos down the side seams, and matching revolver holsters, were certainly not! Members of the 8th Texas Cavalry were also reported to have clothed themselves in bearskin pants. One even had an entire bearskin suit! USAMHI/photo by Jim Enos.

old saw mill blades: 'Some were about twelve inches long [and] one and one half inches wide. Every fellow ground and polished his own ... The scabbards were made of good leather, were sewed and riveted with lead rivets. They were arranged to carry ... on the cartridge belt. Our bayonets were fitted to the muzzle of the guns by Uncle Ranse Horne, who was an ingenious workman ...'.

By the winter of 1861/62, the Lone Star Rifles, Co. L, and possibly the whole of the 1st Texas, were well clothed in uniforms probably purchased under the commutation system, and made up by tailors in Virginia. Photographic evidence points to the fact that an officers' uniform was adopted by the 1st Texas at the same time. Unusually this consisted of a double-breasted coat for company grade officers, following

Men of the 1st Texas Infantry wearing uniforms received whilst at Camp Quantico. Their single-breasted frock coats were fastened with nine large buttons. The collar and pointed cuffs were faced a dark colour, perhaps black, and the cuffs bore a single button on the point. Trousers were also grey with dark seam stripes. Forage caps, with flat tops tilted forward, may have been plain grey, and were ornamented with a small star in the centre, with 'TEXAS' in brass letters curved around the bottom edge. The latter feature was a popular fad throughout the whole army during this winter period, and were more than likely purchased from a sutler than representing any kind of general issue. Rosenburg Library, Galveston, Texas.

Confederate rather than U.S. regulations. Insignia combined the two influences, with Federal shoulder straps and Confederate collar bars.

Regarding the 4th Texas Infantry, the best evidence for the first uniform of the Tom Green Rifles, Co. B, is provided by the ambrotype and recollections of Private Valerius C. Giles. Shortly after enlistment, Giles wrote: 'We were a motley looking set but as a rule, comfortably dressed. In my company we had about four different shades of gray, but all the trimmings were of black braid ... The citizens of Austin and the surrounding neighbourhood bought the cloth. An old tailor took our measurements and cut the uniforms[,] then the ladies made them up. Oh, we were fine!'

In his ambrotype, Giles wears a single-breasted frock coat of grey, a little shorter in the skirts than many of the period, and slightly darker grey trousers with black seam stripes. The coat is trimmed around the collar and down the front edge with black tape. The same braid edges the shoulder straps and cuffs, the latter with a parallel band no more than two inches in from the edge. This garment fastened with seven large buttons.

The Tom Green Rifles wore fatigue caps, but Giles' father insisted that his son purchase for himself 'the best hat on the house', which he wore in his

photo, one brim pinned up with a star bought at the photographer's studio. This impressively large hat, waterproofed with goose grease, lasted Giles until Gaines' Mill in 1862!

The first uniform of the Lone Star Guards, Co. E, was made of 'imported gray cloth,' tailored to individual measurements and sewn by the Ladies Aid Society of the First Methodist Church at Waco. These uniforms were trimmed in dark blue. Based on an image of the Taylor brothers who enlisted in the company, photographic evidence indicates that this uniform consisted of a grey jacket with either 8 or 9 buttons, trimmed around all the collar, edges and cuffs with half-inch wide braid. Grey trousers were also trimmed with a seam stripe of the same material. Black slouch hats were pinned up on one side, probably by metal stars. Both Taylor brothers wore narrow civilian leather belts without accoutrements. Over their shoulders were slung straps of light-colour probably supporting haversacks and canteens.

Evidence suggests that one, if not more, of the companies comprising the 4th Texas originally wore dark blue U.S. army sack coats, and possibly also trousers of the same provenance. Although the Sandy Point Mounted Rifles, also known as the Henderson Guards, enlisted in civilian dress, each man was issued a 'blue sack coat, very full, almost in the shape of a gown,' together with blue trousers, a pair of shoes, two pair of socks, and two shirts, whilst at Camp Van Dorn near Houston. It would seem reasonable to assume that these were large size coats taken over by the state with the capture of Federal military property. Similarly, members of the Grimes County Greys, Co. G, and the Porter Guards, Co. H, were photographed wearing sack coats of dark colour.

Two members of the Grimes County Greys were also photographed between July/August 1861 wearing plain grey frock coats, with darker coloured slouch hats and trousers. Musician Richard Pinckney wore a single breasted seven-button coat, whilst that worn by his brother, Private John M. Pinckney, was double-breasted with two rows of seven buttons.

While the 1st Texas evidently adopted a regimental-style uniform for officers, those in the 4th Texas appear to have chosen a version of the Confederate regulation uniform. An interesting variation appears in a photo of 3rd Lieutenant William D. Rounsavall of the Sandy Point Mounted Rifles, who is shown wearing a plain double-breasted grey frock coat of regulation style with a single gold collar bar and sleeve knot of a single gold braid. Rounsavall's forage cap is also grey, apparently with a gold braid around the top of the band. On the flat crown, brass letters spell out

Private John S. Pickle, Co. B, 18th Texas Cavalry, wears an example of the uniform manufactured at the State Penitentiary at Huntsville during 1862. He holds what seems to be a Whitney Navy Revolver. The butt of another weapon is pushed into his waist belt. PICB07051 Austin History Center, Austin Public Library.

'TEXAS'.

The dress of the 4th Texas' chaplain, Presbyterian minister Nicholas A. Davis is unusually well documented. A correspondent to the *Daily Richmond Enquirer* of 25 September 1861 noted: 'I observed a

The rank of Third Lieutenant James C. Bates, 9th Texas Cavalry, may be indicated by his very long shoulder straps.

USAMHI/photo by Jim Enos.

chaplain (Rev. Nicholas A. Davis, of Texas) in uniform on yesterday, which ... I admired above anything I have yet seen. A suit of black clothing strait (sic) breasted, with one row of brass buttons, and simple pointed cuff with a small olive branch about six inches long, running up the sleeve. We learn that it was made by C. Wendlinger, No. 146, Main st. No stripes on the pants.'

Davis himself complained of the 'exorbitant charges' of Mr. Wendlinger for the 'coat and pants - $45.00 which is a little more than contracted for ...' A photograph of this uniform shows the coat to have had eight buttons, with two small ones on each cuff. The 'olive branch', consisting of a single narrow gold braid, was formed of nine 'leaves' or loops, becoming progressively smaller towards the top. Davis was noted by an eyewitness as wearing a slouch hat.

Grey overshirts of various patterns seem to have been very popular with the 5th Texas. B. Hugh Fuller of the Bayou City Guard, Co. A, was photographed wearing a light grey double-breasted version with falling collar and plastron front secured by two rows of small buttons. The collar, cuffs and plastron were all edged with narrow dark trim, whilst a small five-pointed star also decorated the former. Private James J. Smith of the Dixie Blues, Co. E, was photographed, probably upon enlistment, also wearing a long, grey blouse-shaped hunting shirt which buttoned down the front, with long black patches sewn along the shoulders in imitation of shoulder straps. He also wore a plain black felt hat. Private Andrew Jackson Read wore a plain grey pullover shirt with three buttons down the front, and light grey forage cap with brass letters spelling out his name 'A J READ' on top, when he joined Company F in July 1861. Two soldiers believed to have belonged to the Milam County Greys, Co. G, were photographed wearing similarly-patterned light grey overshirts and trousers with dark seam stripes. To confuse things, the Felder brothers of the Dixie Blues wore single-breasted frock coats and pants of an unmatched shade of grey wool when they were mustered in on 8 August 1861. Their headgear also differed, that of Rufus King Felder being a Model 1861-pattern forage cap, whilst Myers Martindale Felder's was basically a Model 1851 dress cap with stiffening removed. The possible lack of matching clothing in this regiment is best illustrated by the fact that Private John W. Stevens was advised upon enlistment in the Texas Polk Rifles, Co. H, to 'get just what suited his fancy and have it made up in any style he chose - Jes so it was a uniform'!

A member of the 4th Texas wrote of being issued 'tolerably good' overcoats 'with capes on them' in late October 1861. It would seem likely that the whole of Hood's brigade was furnished with winter overcoats at the same time. About this time it was described as being a '... long line of gray. Three thousand bright Texas boys ... with Enfield rifles and bayonets glittering.'

The Texas troops remaining in the Western theatre of the war were far less well served with clothing. The companies and regiments of volunteers assembling in camps of instruction went through a long hot summer not only without receiving arms and uniforms, but without wagons, tents, medicines, and many other necessities. Rip Ford's 2nd Mounted Riflemen were deplorably short of clothing. Since being stationed on the Texas frontier, it had received no contributions from the people of the state. By the fall of 1861 President Lincoln's blockade, though not highly effective, had cut off direct trade through Galveston and other regular ports. One of the first moves of the Military Board established by the legislature in January 1862 was to utilize the State Penitentiary at Huntsville for the manufacture of cloth. Eventually, a tannery and workshops for making shoes and hats were also established. This operation thus became one of the largest cotton and woollen mills in the Confederate southwest. Once produced, this cloth seems to have been cut and tailored into uniforms by local tailor shops working under state contract. A Dallas *Herald* article reported that Company B, 18th Texas Cavalry, was dressed in a 'yellowish-gray tunic coat and pantaloons made of Penitentiary Jeans, with two rows of brass buttons on the front of the coat and a yellow stripe down the side of the pantaloons', when they arrived in that city on 22 January 1862. Penitentiary records show that this company, commanded by Captain H.S. Morgan, was furnished Kersey wool, cotton osnaburg and cotton jeans in December 1861.

Colonel John C. Moore of the 2nd Texas Infantry (also known as the 2nd Texas Sharpshooters) was noted for caring for the welfare of his troops. As a last resort he also took advantage of captured Federal clothing, and issued his 'rag-tag regiment' with dark blue U.S. Army sack coats like those worn within Hood's Brigade in Virginia. The 2nd Texas later received uniforms of undyed wool a few days before leaving Corinth for Shiloh in March 1862. After the battle, a Federal prisoner is reputed to have inquired: 'Who were them hell cats that went into battle dressed in their graveclothes?'

Private Henry D. Hart of Bate's Battalion (Brazoria Coast Regiment), Texas Volunteers, reorganised into the 13th Texas Infantry, was photographed sometime during 1862 wearing another possible example of a uniform made from Penitentiary cloth. Fastened by a single row of eight large buttons, the coat was grey with solid faced collar and cuffs, the latter bearing at least two small buttons sewn along the top seam. One inch wide braid of the same colour was also sewn diagonally from the collar to the shoulder seams, and also along the coat front and around the tails. His cap and pants were made from the same cloth and trimmings. The 16th Texas Infantry was described as being clad in 'wool, and straw hats, homespun pants, and faded penitentiary jackets' in 1863.

Towards the end of 1862 the machinery at the Penitentiary began to wear out and efforts to replace it met with little success. Hence, Texas troops were again without a reliable supply of clothing. The agent for Darnell's 18th Texas Cavalry, dismounted and stationed in northwestern Arkansas, returned to Dallas on 13 September, where he placed in the Herald an urgent request for clothes. Items specified were flannel, linsey, shoes, hats, leather, or additional clothing of 'any description whatever.' He would pay for delivery. Despite such shortages, the British diarist,

This hispanic Confederate from Houston, Texas, has solid facing colour on his collar and cuffs. David Wynn Vaughan.

Lieutenant Colonel Arthur Freemantle, observed a dress parade of the 3rd Texas Infantry on 8 April 1863, and recorded: 'The men were well clothed, though great variety existed in their uniforms. Some companies wore blue, some grey, some had French kepis, others wideawakes and Mexican hats.... During all my travels in the South I never saw a regiment so well clothed or so well drilled as this one, which has never been in action, or exposed to much hardship.'

Six days earlier, Freemantle had found the 14th Cavalry Battalion Partisan Rangers wearing 'flannel shirts, very ancient trousers, jack-boots with enormous spurs, and black felt hats, ornamented with the "lone star of Texas".' The dismounted 2nd Cavalry Regiment (Pyron's) was described during the same period as being 'dressed in every variety of costume, and armed with every variety of weapon.'

Virginia

On the eve of secession, the militia of Virginia was organised territorially into 5 divisions, 28 brigades, and 185 regiments of the line. Each brigade embraced two or more counties and contained four or more regiments. On an average during the years 1851-1860, there were between 125 and 150 active volunteer militia companies of light infantry or riflemen. These belonged either to distinctive Volunteer Militia regiments or battalions, or were formed into a 'Volunteer Battalion' of a line militia regiment. John Brown's Raid on Harper's Ferry, plus rumours of attempts to free the prisoners at Charlestown, prompted a call for approximately 50 Volunteer companies into active state service for various periods of duty during October/November of 1859.

Essentially, the volunteer militia companies of Virginia adopted uniforms of their own choosing during the period prior to the Civil War, despite the fact that a state uniform was prescribed by the militia law of 1858. Detailed in general orders dated May of that year, it was based on 'the regulations of the army of the United States, except that the buttons shall have the Virginia coat of arms thereon.' Other significant differences for cavalry included frock coats, trimmed with yellow, instead of jackets as worn by the regular service. The influence of this state uniform was widespread, as the companies formed after its creation were in theory expected to adopt it. However, plans for a state-wide uniform were further thwarted by the act of 30 March 1860, which once again permitted companies to chose their own style of dress.

Only two Volunteer organisations in the state adopted anything like a regimental uniform. These were the 1st Regiment of Virginia Volunteers, originally organised in 1851, and the 2nd Battalion Virginia Volunteers, established in 1860.

On 5 July 1858 the 7th New York Regiment had visited Richmond, and their smart black-trimmed grey jackets, caps and pants, with white waist and shoulder belts, left a marked impression on their Virginian counterparts who wore a mixture of blue, green and grey. Efforts to prescribe a regimental uniform for the 1st Regiment in the wake of the Seventh's visit initially came to naught; but by July 1859 the *Daily Richmond Enquirer* was able to report: 'The different Companies attached to the First Regiment of Virginia Volunteers

Three members of the Richmond Greys, Co. A, 1st Regiment of Virginia Volunteers, photographed at Charles Town, Virginia, at the time of the hanging of John Brown in December 1859. The sergeant at centre wears the short-skirted frock coat adopted by this company around 1851. The officer at left, and the enlisted man at right, both wear the fatigue jacket adopted in 1859. Russell Hicks Jr.

... are almost all adopting the gray uniform. Even the Irish and German companies are throwing off their characteristic styles of national dress, and are adopting the American gray...'

Although a detailed description of the regimental full dress chosen by the 1st Regiment has not survived, a reconstruction of it is possible based on the changes which occurred in company dress during the period prior to the Civil War. From available evidence it seems that most of these companies adopted a black cloth, or beaverskin, 'National Guard'-style dress cap with pompon; grey cloth fatigue cap with black band; grey frock coat trimmed according to company preference; grey shirt and black overcoat. With the exception of the Virginia Rifles and the Howitzers, all companies wore white webbing cross belts. The former retained their black cross belts, whilst the Howitzer Company preferred only a white waist belt for their sabres.

The Richmond Grays, Co. A, of this regiment had been wearing a grey uniform based on that of the 7th New York since their organisation in 1844. About 1851, the short-skirted frock coat replaced the coatee. Also the National Guard-style dress cap, as worn by the 7th New York, with black felt body and black patent leather strips at top and bottom, with white pompon, was adopted. By 1859, the Grays also had items of undress uniform including a nine-button grey fatigue jacket with belt loops, and black edging on a low collar, black shoulder straps; grey forage cap with black oilskin covers, and 'RG' in brass letters on the front. New grey frock coats of the long-skirted pattern were procured in early 1861.

The Richmond City Guard, Co. B (originally called the Fireside Protectors, and also later known as Lee's Riflemen, after their second commanding officer), adopted a plain grey frock coat with 'gold braid rectangles' on the collar and gold epaulette keeps, after their organisation in December 1860.

The Montgomery Guard, Co. C, paraded for the first time in their 'newly adopted grey uniform' on 4 July 1859, on which occasion the *Richmond Enquirer* reported that it 'looks neat, fits well, and though it is grey, is more preferable to the eye, than the marked abundance of vivid green that formerly characterized the style of the gallant Montgomeries'. The latter is a reference to the full dress worn by this unit before 1859, which consisted of a green coatee with three rows of buttons, trimmed with gold lace and faced with buff collar, cuffs and coat tails; sky-blue pants with one and a half-inch buff seam stripe; and green M1851 dress cap with buff band. This uniform continued in use for special occasions throughout

Private John Werth, Richmond Howitzers, Co. H, 1st Regiment of Virginia Volunteers, wearing the dark grey fatigue jacket adopted by this company in 1861. Werth probably left the Howitzers in May of that year to form a Home Guard unit called the Richmond Mounted City Guard. Eleanor S. Brockenbrough Library, The Museum of the Confederacy, Richmond, Virginia.

1860.

Organised on 23 June 1859 under Richmond attorney Randolph Milton Cary, the great aim of F Company was 'to build up a regiment in imitation of the "National Guard" of New York'. Hence, they chose a full dress consisting of a long-skirted 'cadet grey' frock coat with collar edged black, and black worsted epaulettes with white fringe, and white cord inside the crescent. Pants were also grey with two-inch wide black seam stripes. Headgear consisted of the National Guard-style dress cap. This company also adopted a fatigue jacket, cap and trousers similar to that of the Grays.

By 1861 the dress uniform of F Company had been revised somewhat. As later described by John H. Worsham, who joined the unit that year: 'This company had a fine cadet gray uniform. It consisted first of a frock coat which had a row of Virginia fire-gilt buttons on its front. Around the cuff of the sleeve was a band of gold braid and two small fire-gilt buttons. On the collar the same gold braid was so arranged that it looked very much like the mark of rank for a first lieutenant which was afterwards adopted by the Confederacy. The pants had a black stripe about one and a quarter inches wide along the outer seams. The cap was made of the same cadet gray cloth, trimmed with black braid and two small fire-gilt buttons. On its front was the letter F. The non-commissioned officers had their mark of rank worked on the sleeves of their coats with black braid.'

The Richmond Light Infantry Blues, Co. E, were normally resplendent in their dark blue coatee with white cassimere collar, cuffs and plastron front; blue trousers with white seam stripe; and blue cloth cap with pompon - but by February 1861 had adopted their grey regimental uniform with long-skirted frock coat.

Company G, commanded by Captain William Gordon, was originally organised in July 1859, and by February 1860 paraded in 'full uniform and undress cap', consisting of a nine-button grey frock coat, with collar edged with black braid and decorated with a gold loop; grey trousers with broad black seam stripes; and a grey forage cap with black band and brass letter 'G' on the front. By August 1860 this company had also acquired an 'undress uniform' which included a 'Fatigue Jacket.'

Formed on 9 November 1859, the Howitzer Company, which later expanded into a battalion known as the Richmond Howitzers, initially assembled during January 1860 in 'red shirt, grey pants, [and miscellaneous] fatigue cap.' During the following month, they acquired a 'full dress uniform' from 'Stagg's', and 'dress caps from Ellet & Weisiger.' The former consisted of a grey frock coat with 'wings', whilst the latter was presumably a version of the 'National Guard' dress cap. Grey fatigue caps with red

F Company, 1st Regiment of Virginia Volunteers, wearing the uniform adopted in 1861. From photographs and descriptions by Richard Warren.

band and gilt letter 'H', their company designation within the 1st Regiment, on the front, were being worn by October 1860. By the beginning of the Civil War, the Howitzer Battalion had a dark grey fatigue jacket with belt loops, and red wool piping around collar and shoulder straps.

The Virginia Rifles, Co. K, laid their blue and green dress uniforms aside, and appeared on parade in 'new gray uniforms, with black cross belts and shoulder straps' on 12 April 1860.

The Armory Band, under the leadership of James B. Smith, became the regimental band of the First in April 1860, and members were photographed wearing long-skirted plain grey frock coats, grey chasseur-pattern forage caps with dark bands, and darker, possibly blue trousers with narrow, light-coloured seams stripes.

It seems that most companies received 'new Regimental overcoats' during January 1860. According to J.H. Worsham, F Company 'had black cloth overcoats - the skirt reaching a little below the knees, the capes a little below the elbow - and the buttons

Private Henry A. Tarrall, Woodis Riflemen. Organised at Norfolk, Virginia, in 1858, this company wore a dark green frock coat with black velvet front, collar, and shoulder patches, trimmed with gold cord. Pants were also green with black stripes edged with gold. A red pompon is pinned to his black Hardee hat. From a private collection. The Museum of the Confederacy, Richmond, Virginia.

Charles A. Pace of the Danville Blues, a light infantry volunteer company organised in 1841. This unit became Company A, 18th Virginia Infantry. Probably photographed in 1861, Pace wears full dress which includes fountain plume, tail-coat, and white gloves. Eleanor S. Brockenbrough Library, The Museum of the Confederacy, Richmond, Virginia.

were Virginia-gilt.'

The 2nd Battalion Virginia Volunteers was formed in Spotsylvania County during the spring of 1860, when the Fredericksburg Rifle Grays, Washington Guards, and the Coleman Guards - all of Fredericksburg - were detached from the 16th Regiment, Virginia Militia. On 23 April of that year the Richmond *Daily Dispatch* announced: 'The Fredericksburg (Va.) volunteer companies have adopted the gray uniform of the Richmond Regiment.'

With the secession of Virginia on 7 April, the older Volunteer Militia companies, including the 1st Regiment of Volunteers, were enrolled for active state service. By late July 1861, the uniforms of the First, which presumably included a mixture of grey frock coats and fatigue jackets, had seen hard wear on the 'plains of Manassas' and, according to regimental historian Charles T. Loehr, were 'somewhat in need of repairs.' Even the Drum Corps was in need of new jackets and pants. On 9 September 1861 the Richmond City Council appropriated $50,000 in order to supply volunteers from the city with winter clothing. The First was probably in receipt of new uniforms via

Drum Major Charles Rudolph M. von Pohle, of the 1st Regiment of Virginia Volunteers. He wore a grey frock coat with black plastron front and gold lace braid linking three rows of ten gilt buttons; grey trousers with gold lace seam stripe; red sash trimmed with blue; and tall bearskin cap topped with a large red, white and blue pompon. His Drum Corps, consisting of sixteen boys over the age of 16, was organised during April 1860 and paraded at the head of the 1st Regiment 'attired in red jackets and white pants' on 31 May 1860. From a photograph by Ron Field.

this source by late October. An ambrotype of Hampden Pleasants Hay of the Richmond City Guard, and L.R. Wingfield of the Old Dominion Guard, taken sometime before the former was sent on detached service, shows two men from different companies in the regiment wearing an identical uniform, possibly based on the fatigue dress adopted before the war by the Richmond Greys and F Company. Hay and Wingfield wear an eight-button grey fatigue jacket with black tape trim around the edges of the collar, and black shoulder flaps. Their trousers are plain grey, and tucked into boots, possibly indicating winter wear. Hay holds a dark-coloured forage cap with a gilt letter 'B' on top.

The pattern of fatigue jacket issued to the 1st Regiment of Virginia Volunteers in October 1861 may well have influenced the Confederate Clothing Bureau, established in Richmond earlier during August of that year, in its decision to produce the short-waisted 'shell jacket' as part of the uniform supplied by the Quartermaster Department to troops in Confederate service throughout the remainder of the Civil War.

Regarding the countless other Virginia companies which volunteered for Confederate service during the summer of 1861, their uniforms were generally composed of a mixture of frock coats, jackets, tail-coats, and 'hunting shirts,' varying in colour from grey, blue, green, black and red. Headgear variously consisted of dress caps, forage caps, 'Sicilian' caps, slouch hats, and Mexican War hats.

Much of the cloth for these uniforms was procured from the Crenshaw Woollen Company of Richmond, which had been converted from a flour mill in 1860 by Lewis D. Crenshaw. This firm produced 'Fine Cassimeres and Cloths of every variety, from Fine Virginia Merino and Mestizo wool.' It began by producing 'Army Cloths, ... at first expressly for the Virginia Military Academy' in 1861. Kelly, Tackett & Ford of Manchester, Virginia, produced a variety of goods, including red flannel and some light blue cloth. The Scotsville Manufacturing Company, and Bonsack & Whitmore, both produced large quantities of woollen jeans. Material of various colours was also obtained from a Staunton mill, whilst the Swartz Woollen Mills at Waterloo supplied cloth for the troops from Culpeper County and vicinity.

Typical of the goods available for military companies to purchase on the eve of secession was that advertised for sale in 1860 by Kent, Paine & Co., of Richmond: '60 pieces Medium and fine Blue Cloths, 250 pieces Blue and Grey Satinets; Army Clothes; Green Clothes, for Rifle Corps; Medium and Extra

Military Buttons; Gauntlets; Gilt and Worsted Braids and Cords...' By April 1861, this firm was offering 'Grey Cassimeres, manufactured in Maryland, Virginia and Georgia.'

Early in the war, hunting shirts were particularly popular among the companies which made up the 11th Virginia Infantry, raised mainly in Lynchburg. Commonly referred to today as a 'fireman's shirt', this garment consisted of an overshirt with falling collar, pointed cuff facings, and a double-breasted front panel, or removable plastron. The Home Guard, raised by Samuel Garland, Jr. during November 1859 in response to John Brown's Raid on Harper's Ferry, originally chose a dark blue frock coat and pants based on the 1858 state regulations, 'substituting the cap for the Hungarian [Hardee] hat.' However, by April 1860 they wore a 'fatigue uniform' composed of a 'blue flannel hunting shirt, with red breast and collar, trimmed with light blue, black pants and blue cap.' The Home Guard volunteered under Captain Kirkwood Otey as Co. G, 11th Virginia, in May 1861.

The Lynchburg Rifles were raised among the faculty and students of Lynchburg College during the spring of 1861. On 1 May the *Lynchburg Daily Virginian* reported: 'The Lynchburg Rifles are progressing well in their drills. They promise to make a fine company. Their uniforms are being made and will soon be completed. They are of gray goods trimmed with blue and will look well.' Based on photographic evidence, this uniform consisted of a grey hunting shirt with dark blue collar, plastron, and cuffs with a single small button sewn at the point. When unbuttoned and removed, the plastron front revealed three broad, vertical, possibly light blue, bands of silk or polished cotton trim. On some shirts a small patch of the same material appears to have been sewn along the top of the shoulders, in imitation of a shoulder strap. The shirt front could, in turn, be unbuttoned and fastened back forming two wide lapels. The forage cap worn by the Lynchburg Rifles was grey with a dark, probably blue, band. Their trousers were also grey with dark one-inch seam stripes. Commanded by Captain James E. Blankenship, this unit became Co. E of the 11th Virginia.

The Lynchburg Rifle Greys, Co. A of this regiment, were organised on 23 January 1860, and elected Maurice Langhorne as their captain. The following day, the *Daily Virginian* announced: 'The uniform of the company willl be made in Virginia of Virginia goods, the cloth being manufactured at Staunton; the suit made by our tailors; and the caps by Sinzer.' Members of this company were photographed wearing

Lynchburg Rifles, Co. E, 11th Virginia Infantry, with plastron fronts removed. From photographs by Ron Field.

a grey hunting shirt similar to that of the Lynchburg Rifles. The collar, plastron and cuffs were possibly dark blue or black. Once the plastron was removed, the shirt probably had narrow bands of dark braid running vertically up the front, parallel with, and outside, the two rows of buttons. The Rifle Greys also wore grey forage caps with dark bands, with the letters 'RG' on the front. Their pants were grey with broad seam stripes.

The Southern Guards from Yellow Branch, Campbell County, were reported by the Petersburg *Daily Express* of 4 May 1861 to be wearing 'black jackets; [and] grey pants with black stripes.' According to surviving photographs, this may be interpreted as meaning a grey hunting shirt faced with black collar, plastron, and cuffs. Caps were grey with black bands, and the letters 'SG' in front. At least four members of this company were photographed wearing large 'secession cockades' pinned to their plastron fronts.

The Fincastle Rifles, Co. D, 11th Virginia, were formed during December 1859, and hastily donned a 'fanciful uniform' described in the Alexandria *Gazette* as being 'a plain linsey hunting shirt - black and red.' This was subsequently described by the *Frank Leslie's Illustrated Newspaper* correspondent reporting the execution of John Brown's accomplices at Charlestown as being 'a most picturesque uniform, being half Scotch' in style. The artist accompanying him illustrated this as a plaid, or tartan hunting shirt, together with 'green baise cape', plumed slouch hat, and knee-high stockings!

Other Lynchburg companies wearing hunting shirts made by the tailors and ladies of the city included the Lynchburg Artillery and the Beauregard Rifles, temporarily known as 'the Zouaves'. Regarding the former, artilleryman James McCanna was photographed sometime between late April and May 1861 wearing a grey shirt with plastron front removed showing herring bone-pattern trim, possibly red in colour. Cuffs and collar were also in the same facing colour. The Beauregard Rifles, also known as the Lynchburg Beauregards, who later re-organised as Captain Marcellus N. Moorman's Company, Virginia Horse Artillery, were described as wearing 'gray pantaloons, gray shirts with green front, trimmed with black, and navy caps' soon after organisation in April 1861. Upon their arrival in Richmond, the *Dispatch* reported them as having 'a peculiar red cap', which may bear witness to a continued 'zouave' influence. An unknown member of this unit was photographed with his green plastron removed revealing four narrow, vertical bands of black trim running from neck to waist. Collar and pointed cuffs were also faced with the same material.

Elsewhere in the state, the Appomatox Invincibles, who enlisted as Co. A, 44th Virginia Infantry on 26 April 1861, adopted a uniform of cloth made by the Crenshaw Woollen Mills, designed by company member First Lieutenant John M. Steptoe, consisting of 'gray pants with black stripes one inch-wide, a gray shirt with collar to turn down or throw open and trimmed with black cord. The cap also will be gray

Thomas B. Horton enlisted as a sergeant in the Southern Guards, Co. B, 11th Virginia Infantry, and was promoted to captain in April 1862. The fact that he carries a sword here would indicate that he received his dark grey hunting shirt with satinette plastron front around that time. Note the patches on his shoulders, and white dress gloves. Eleanor S. Brockenbrough Library, The Museum of the Confederacy, Richmond, Virginia.

with a black band. The pants and shirt to be held to the waist with a patent lether [sic] belt with brass plate in front.'

During the Fall of 1860, two military companies

Private Richard Henry Toler (right) of the Lynchburg Home Guard received his hunting shirt, possibly from the same source as Captain Horton, before being detailed on signal telegraph duty with E. P. Alexander in November 1861. Murray Forbes Taylor (left) also served under Alexander as an adjutant. Russell Hicks, Jr.

An unidentified member of the 11th Virginia Infantry. Wearing a hunting shirt very similar to that of the Lynchburg Rifle Greys, he is armed with a M1842 'Mississippi' Rifle, revolver, Sheffield-type Bowie knife, drum canteen, and rigid box knapsack, complete with waterproof blanket roll. Russell Hicks, Jr.

were formed by the students of the University of Virginia. The Southern Guards, under Captain E. S. Hutter, wore a light blue pullover shirt fastened with three small buttons, and trimmed with dark blue around a low standing collar, pocket, buttoned front and cuffs. Their high-crowned forage caps were grey and quartered with black piping. Trousers were originally to be black, but an ambrotype of company member Henry Mitchie and friend shows grey pants with wide black seam stripes. The Sons of Liberty, commanded by Captain J. T. Toch, wore 'red shirts.'

In Richmond, the 179th Regiment Virginia Militia, embracing all of the city east of 10th Street, had taken steps to arm and clothe some of its companies for possible active service during February 1861. On the fourth of that month, it was recommended that the uniform of the regiment should consist of a 'Blue flannel cloth hunting shirt with blue fringe and Virginia buttons: pants, dark (civilian).' It is not known

how far this recommendation was acted upon, or how many of its companies were thus clothed. However, the Fireside Protectors, raised during January 1861 and subsequently known as the Virginia Life Guard, were attached to the 179th as 'a uniformed company of the line', and later volunteered for state service as Co. B, 15th Virginia Infantry wearing a uniform of this description, also manufactured at the Crenshaw Woollen Mills.

Virginia cavalry companies were particularly fond of wearing hunting shirts. That worn by James Henry Woodson of the Appomatox Rangers, Co. H, 2nd Virginia Cavalry, was grey with light-coloured plastron, collar and cuffs. William Worsley Mead of the Loudon Cavalry, Co. K, 6th Virginia Cavalry, wore a plain grey shirt trimmed with narrow braid around edges, collar and pockets. That worn by Bladen Dulany Lake of the Mountain Rangers, Co. A, 7th Virginia Cavalry, was grey faced with black in a

James Henry Woodson, Appomattox Rangers, Co. H, 2nd Virginia Cavalry, wears a uniform similar to that of the Lynchburg companies. Woodson's unit was raised in Appomattox County but was mustered into state service at Lynchburg. Hence he was probably outfitted there. Russell Hicks, Jr.

Private Andrew Jackson Lawson, Red House Volunteers, Co. A, 21st Virginia Infantry, in another version of a plastron-fronted hunting shirt. Russell Hicks, Jr.

broad band of facing colour running down its buttoned front, and on collar, cuffs, and pocket tops.

Other Virginia cavalry units seem to have clung to their pre-war dress when they entered Confederate service. The Amelia Light Dragoons (Co. G) and the Loudon Light Horse (Co. H), 1st Virginia Cavalry, continued to wear their dark blue 1858 state regulation uniforms well into the summer of 1861. The latter took part in the charge on the 11th New York (Ellsworth's Fire Zouaves) at First Manassas. The Wise Troop, of Lynchburg, named after ex-Governor Henry A. Wise, was formed during November 1859, and adopted 'red coats', 'bright blue pants with a gold cord down the sides', and helmets with 'the brightest scarlet horsehair tufts hanging down behind them.' Later, during July 1861, and after this unit had entered war service as Co. B, 2nd Virginia Cavalry, the *New York Times* reported that 'a uniform coat taken from a secession captain [John S. Langhorne] of the "Wise Cavalry"' was on exhibition in Philadelphia. It was further described as being 'scarlet faced with black velvet, on which are two rows of bell buttons, on the face of which are the Virginia arms with the motto "Sic semper tyrannis." It was a curious looking uniform, and as lining was scarce in "the land of cotton," it was patched up with common bolting cloth.'

This Virginian wears a hunting shirt which was tinted red with pale blue trim in the original image. David Wynn Vaughan collection.

The Botetourt Dragoons, raised at Fincastle during January 1861 under Captain Andrew L. Pitzer, adopted a 'blue cloth suit, trimmed with yellow', which may be a further reference the 1858 state uniform. During July 1861, the Boston *Courier* reported the seizure of 'a coat and cap belonging to the Old Dominion Dragoons [Co. B, 3rd Virginia Cavalry].' Taken by members of the Wightman Rifles, 4th Regiment Massachusetts Militia, near Fortress Monroe, they were described as follows: 'The material from which they are manufactured is heavy blue satinet, far superior in quality to the material of the clothing of our troops. The coat is strongly, though not handsomely, made. The cap, of ordinary army pattern, was made at Norfolk by W. H. C. Lovitt, and, judging from this specimen, the Massachusetts volunteers, when they capture that city, will find him a good mand to patronize. It is ornamented with cross sabres in front, and bears in large brass letter, the initials of the company's name, "O.D.D." The coat appears to have seen some service, but is almost as good as new. A mischevious contemporary suggested that the coat be shown to the contractors for clothing for our volunteers.'

The Prince William Cavalry, who became Co. A, 4th Virginia Cavalry, proudly enlisted on 17 April 1861 in a uniform of grey cloth made at Kelly's Mills in Culpeper County, which consisted of 'a frock coat with one row of buttons up the front and one each side; connecting at the top with a gold lace V.' They also wore grey pants with 'yellow stripes, black hats with black plumes on the left side held up with crossed sabers and a shield with the letters PWC in front - a neat uniform in which the most insignificant must look his best ...'

The first uniform of the Little Fork Rangers, also of Culpeper County, was: 'beautiful and conspicuous - red, white, blue and yellow. They would have furnished a splendid target for Yankee bullets, had they worn them into battle, but fortunately they did not. Blue caps, red cut-away jackets with yellow stripes designated their branch of service - cavalry. This was their uniform during the summer and fall of 1860. During the winter and early spring of 1861, they wore black trousers with a red stripe down the seam.'

After the secession of Virginia on 7 April 1861, the Rangers purchased grey cloth from the Swartz Mills at Waterloo, which was cut by a tailor at Warrenton and put together into uniforms by the ladies of the neighbourhood. They went on to become Co. D of the 4th Virginia Cavalry.

This shirt was worn by Private Kennedy Palmer, Fort Loudon Guards, Co. H, 13th Virginia Infantry. It was grey with solid red trim on collar and cuffs. The Museum of the Confederacy, Richmond, Virginia.

Regarding early war artillery uniforms, the Bedford Light Artillery made 'a fine appearance' in their uniform made 'of dark blue material, the coat buttoning straight up the front, fastened at the waist by a belt, with a short skirt below it.' The pants and coat were trimmed with red with 'a cap to match, mounted with two brass cannon crossed obliquely.'

The zouave influence was represented in Virginia by the Richmond Zouaves, who organised under Captain Edward McConnell, Jr. during May 1861. Their uniforms were made by the ladies of the Monumental Episcopal Church, and were probably based on a typical colourful zouave pattern, consisting of a blue jacket and orange baggy trousers. On 10 June, the Richmond *Daily Whig* published the following by 'Le Zouave', an anonymous member of the unit: 'At drill hours our Armory [Corinthian Hall] presents quite an animated scene, and uniforms other than the blue and orange, mingle *cum toga civile*. Tonight, two of the Zouaves Francais were present and expressed themselves well pleased at our appearance and movements. All thanks to the courteous Frenchmen, whether we deserve the compliments or not.'

Presumably the latter is a reference to members of Coppen's Battalion of Louisiana Zouaves who had arrived in the city three days earlier. A complete zouave uniform, which possibly belonged to an officer of the Richmond Zouaves, survives in the collection of the Chicago Historical Society. The navy blue jacket is edged with interwoven gold braid, and is fastened together at the neck by two small buttons or studs secured through a small gold edged tab. The sleeves are decorated with a white clover-leaf design outlined with gold braid, and are slashed and buttoned at the underseam by six small brass buttons bearing the Virginia state seal. The scarlet pants with gold braid seam stripes are in the chasseur-style, being gathered at the waist with pleats, and below the knee into narrow cuffs fastened by buckles or buttons. The chasseur-pattern forage cap is scarlet with gold piping and Hungarian knot on the crown. The blue wool cumberbund has a short scarlet fringe.

The Richmond Zouaves also adopted leggings of white ducking which F. Thomas of Richmond

The Sussex Light Dragoons, Co. H, 13th Virginia Cavalry, adopted a plain grey woollen shirt with small, rectangular plastron secured by four buttons on each side. Headgear consisted of a high-crowned dark blue forage cap, quartered with yellow piping, with the gilt letters 'SLD' over crossed sabres in front. The man at centre has a light-coloured seam stripe just visible on his trousers. Eleanor S. Brockenbrough Library, The Museum of the Confederacy, Richmond, Virginia.

Captain Edward Sixtus Hutter commanded a company of students raised at the University of Virginia called the Southern Guard. Note the secession cockade pinned to the side of his oil skin-covered cap. Russell Hicks, Jr.

undertook to make for 75 cents a pair. However when Captain McConnell called to collect them, Thomas refused to hand the goods over claiming that he had charged $1.50 a pair. McConnell handed over the extra cash, but subsequently hauled Thomas through the Mayor's Court on charges of fraudently obtaining '$5.00, one roll of ducking, and one gross of buckles'!

By 6 September 1861, a C. S. Quartermaster Department Clothing Bureau had been set up in Richmond, and Virginians became some of the first troops in Confederate service to receive supplies of clothing from the central government. This source of clothing continued to be supplemented by the efforts of various ladies aid societies across the state. A supply of state manufactured clothing was particularly essential for those troops not in Confederate service. Units making up the Virginia State Line, established on 15 May 1862, were clothed purely on this basis. A Quartermaster Depot established at Wytheville under

When Chastain B. Clark enlisted in the Lynchburg Rifles, Co. E, 11th Virginia Infantry, in July 1861, he received this shell jacket with unusual seam on the cuffs, and Mexican War-style hat. He holds a Colt M1860 fluted Army revolver and M1842 musket. Russell Hicks, Jr.

Captain J. B. Goodloe had, by 27 December 1862, manufactured the following articles: '6,912 shirts, 6,708 drawers, 3,368 jackets, 3,960 pants, 1,897 overcoats, 1,764 military caps.' In his 1862 report, Quartermaster General L. R. Smoots remarked: 'No efforts or expense have been spared on the part of this office, to supply the wants of the state line troops.'

A Richmond Zouave, Co. E, 44th Virginia Infantry. From artefacts and descriptions by Ron Field.

Arkansas

Throughout the decade prior to the Civil War, the enrolled, or non-uniformed, militia of Arkansas was divided into two divisions: the First being designated to the western portion of the state with its Indian frontier, while the Second embraced the remainder. Within each county, the militia laws authorised the formation of four uniformed volunteer militia companies: one each of artillery, cavalry, infantry and light infantry. Most counties were devoid of such commands, but by 1860 a few, like Phillips and Pulaski, had one or more volunteer companies of reasonably long standing. In Pulaski County these included the Capital Guards, established around 1840;

Company H, 3rd Regiment State Infantry, photographed at Arkadephia in June 1861. No two men are dressed alike. They wear pullover shirts of various cuts and shades, some with trim of different colours around the pockets, cuffs and collars. All wear slouch hats, and at least thirty hold D-guard Bowie knives or large side knives. Many have tin cups attached to their belts, and wear what appear to be canvas packs on their backs. The man second row from the front wears sunglasses, whilst a black Confederate volunteer stands in the fourth row, fourth from the right! General Sweeny's Museum, Republic, Missouri.

Second Lieutenant, Fort Smith Rifles, Co. A or D, 3rd Arkansas State Infantry (left); Color Sergeant, Belle Point Guards, 5th Arkansas State Infantry (centre); Sergeant, Davis Blues, Co. F, 5th Arkansas State Infantry (right). From photographs by Ron Field.

the Pulaski Lancers, a mounted company under Captain Thomas J. Churchill; and the Totten Artillery commanded by Captain W. E. Woodruff, Jr. These companies were permitted to select and procure their own uniforms in whatever style and colour they saw fit to choose.

In addition to this, the Arkansas Military Institute had existed at Tulip, in Dallas County, since 1850. Modelled on the Virginia Military Institute, it apparently adopted the grey dress and fatigue uniforms of that revered establishment. Its doors were closed in 1861 as the cadets under Captain James B. Williamson formed Co. I, 4th Arkansas Infantry.

On 21 January 1861, Governor Henry M. Rector approved two acts of the legislature which reorganised the militia, and placed Arkansas in a more defensible position. The raising of further volunteer companies was encouraged, and moves were made to arm them, especially those units being formed along the western borders of the state. At the same time the legislature

ruled that militia officers were to wear the same uniform as the U.S. Army, 'except commissioned officers of companies, who shall be allowed to adopt any uniform which they may see proper.'

Arkansas was largely unprepared to manufacture uniforms when secession took place on 6 May 1861. The only clothing factory was situated at Nashville in the far southwest corner of the state. Hence, virtually all the clothing supplied to regiments raised in 1861 was improvised and largely homemade. The Military Board established on 15 May, with Governor Rector as president, created the Army of Arkansas, a force comprising the 1st through 5th State Regiments enlisted for six months state defense. These regiments embraced most of the former volunteer militia, who mostly enlisted in their various pre-War uniforms. Second Lieutenant Decatur McDonald of the Fort Smith Rifles, Co. D, 3rd Regiment State Infantry, was photographed in a short-skirted grey frock coat, darker grey trousers, and plumed hat pinned up on the right. Others in his company wore grey coats and pants trimmed with buff braid. Private Clem McCulloch of the Van Buren Frontier Guards, in the same regiment, was pictured on 18 May 1861 wearing a nine-button dark grey, or blue, sack coat with turned-down collar, and rectangular U.S. 'eagle' plate

The Totten Battery, later renamed the Pulaski Battery, was organised by William E. Woodruff, Jr., in 1860. Lieutenant Omar Weaver (left) was killed at Wilson's Creek. An unidentified member of the Pulaski Battery (right). Note the letters 'P' and 'B' either side of the cross cannon on his cap. This company was dressed in 'gray jeans, and carried knapsacks' in 1861. General Sweeny's Museum, Republic, Missouri.

fastening his waist belt.

Judging by the uniform worn by Sergeant Simeon McCown when he posed for an ambrotype during the summer of 1861, the Davis Blues, raised in Nashville, Arkansas, by Captain A. S. Cabell, were particularly well clothed. Designated Co. F of the 5th State Infantry, this company's uniform was probably made at the factory at that place. His grey woollen frock coat was trimmed with either dark blue or black braid across the chest, collar and sleeves.

Colour Sergeant Paul Richard Krone, of the Belle Point Guards, a company of the 5th State Infantry raised among the German population of Fort Smith, was photographed wearing a dark blue frock coat, mid-blue trousers, and holding a M1851 dark blue dress cap with brass letters 'BPG' topped with feather plume. His rank was indicated by three inverted chevrons on each upper arm. John H. Rivers of the

Centerpoint Riflemen, also of the Fifth, recalled: 'We had Uniforms made at home, all alike, the shirts were made of hickory checks, and had red stripes across the breast, five in number: And the pants were out of some thin goods: They were blue, and had red stripes on the outside of each leg, about an inch wide: We were proud of Our Uniforms.'

The 1st Arkansas Volunteer Infantry (Fagan's), raised for 12 months Confederate service at the same time as the State Regiments, wore uniforms of equally great variety. The Eldorado Sentinels, Co. A, were 'well uniformed' in neat grey caps and frock coats, with black cap band, collar and cuffs. Twenty-four men from this unit left home without these items, and were 'uniformed in Virginia at [their] own expense.' Taking advantage of earlier state legislature permitting company grade officers to choose their own uniforms, Captain Charles S. Stark, commanding the Clark County Volunteers, Co. B, chose to wear a light grey coat trimmed, apparently, in light blue, while his light blue pants carried a gold stripe. His coat had three rows of nine buttons, with three small buttons up the front of the cuffs. His company possibly wore a similar uniform. The Camden Knights, Co. C, wore dark blue caps, pants and hunting shirts, the latter cut in varying styles, either plain or with light blue trim. The letters

Second Lieutenant David Alexander, Napoleon Rifles, Co. G, 1st Arkansas Mounted Rifles, wears a multi-coloured plaid shirt over a fancy pleated dress shirt. A secession cockade and feathers decorate his hat. Alexander was cashiered in August 1861 for stabbing to death a member of his own company. General Sweeny's Museum, Republic, Missouri.

Private C.F. Wrenfrey, 1st Arkansas State Cavalry, enlisted in May 1861. He wears a nine-button 'roundabout', or shell jacket, with shoulder straps, and holds a Smith and Wesson revolver, a weapon popular with Confederates early in the war. General Sweeny's Museum, Republic, Missouri.

'CK' occasionally embroidered on their cap fronts were a personalised touch. The Jacksonport Guards, Co. G, adopted light grey caps and trousers, with black cap bands and seam stripes. Their dark grey blouses had the company initials 'JG' appliqued on

either side of the breast in black cloth capital letters. In line with state legislature regarding officers above company grade, Colonel James F. Fagan wore a dark blue frock coat with two rows of five buttons and federal style shoulder straps, and a French-style forage cap with gold rank braid.

The 6th Arkansas Infantry, raised at Little Rock by Colonel Richard Lyon during June 1861, spent most of its time in the western theatre of the war. The City Guard, Co. H, from Camden, enlisted in 'gray roundabout and pants trimmed with red', and 'glazed caps.' William Shores, of this company, was photographed wearing a black Mexican War-pattern cap. The Ouchita Grays, Co. K, wore 'gray roundabouts and pants trimmed with green', with glazed caps.

An attempt to overcome the lack of uniformity within these regiments, and probably even within some companies, was observed by a correspondent of the *Register* of Rock Island, Illinois, on 11 September 1861: 'The uniform of the Confederate army [of the

These three Arkansians wear a variety of fatigue and civilian shirts. Private James McDavid Flynt (left), 2nd Arkansas Infantry, was killed at Murfreesboro. Private William Martin Flynt (centre), 2nd Arkansas Infantry, died 25 July 1865. Private John Harrison Raleigh (right), 11th Arkansas Infantry, was captured at Island No. 10. Note the small heart-shaped patch sewn on his breast. General Sweeny's Museum, Republic, Missouri.

West] is multiform. They are not uniformed at all, and generally speaking , it is impossible to distinguish a Colonel from a private. The only mark of distinction about them, except for their arms, is a piece of flannel stitched to the left shoulder. I was told that white flannel was the distinguishing mark of the troops, yellow that of Arkansas, red that of Louisiana, and so on. Of course this only applies to the Southwest.'

On 15 July 1861, the Military Board agreed to transfer Arkansas commands to the Confederacy. On this occasion it was also agreed that the state should furnish its men with clothing, in return for which it would be recompensed by the War Department at commutation rates. During the following month, the Military Board sent circular letters to all counties asking for citizens to collect clothing for the soldiers and turn it over to the county judge, clerk or sheriff. The Board proposed to pay citizens for the clothing

Private Thomas Bolding, 24th Arkansas Infantry (Portlock's), wears an unusual shell jacket. Fastened by five large gilt buttons, it has buttoned-down pockets on each breast - reminiscent of jackets issued to some Georgia troops.
General Sweeny's Museum, Republic, Missouri.

received with Arkansas or Confederate bonds. The Crockett Rifles, Co. H, 1st Arkansas (Fagan's), named after their original commander Captain Robert H. Crockett, left home without arms or uniforms. Company member Wiley A. Washburn, recalled: 'We immediately proceed[ed] to Va. Stoped [sic] at Lynchburg[,] recd our uniforms and guns. The cloth was bou[g]ht by funds recd from the State.'

Various volunteer aid societies throughout the state supplemented the efforts of the Military Board. Organisations like the Randolph County Central Committee raised funds and purchased 'equipment for volunteers', which was sent on to Governor Rector. Sometimes, committees devoted their labours to one particular company. The Union County Central Committee purchased 'provisions, clothing, [and] arms' specifically for the Lisbon Invincibles, a unit which became Co. I, 6th Arkansas Volunteer Infantry. The citizens of Hempstead supplied the Southern Defenders, a Home Guard company, with 'one coat;

two pairs of pants; two pairs of socks; and two pairs of drawers.' Gold medals were awarded to encourage the state's womenfolk to make cloth. During a period of four months, Mrs. Sallie Bangs, a widow of Sulphur Springs, wove 'a hundred and eight yards of jeans and seventy-eight yards of plain cloth ... also she made cloth for her son who was in the army.'

Possibly following the lead of other states in the Confederacy, the Board also established workshops for the manufacture of uniforms and equipage at the state penitentiary on the outskirts of Little Rock, where the capitol building now stands. By 18 November 1861, a committee was able to report to the legislature that the penitentiary had fabricated for the army 3,000 uniforms, 8,000 pairs of shoes, 250 wagons, 100 sets of wagon and artillery harness, 500 drums, 200 tents, 600 knapsacks and 500 cartridge boxes. Virtually every member of Fagan's 1st Arkansas were in receipt of 'a new uniform, coarse but serviceable', possibly supplied via this source, by November 1861. The usual clothing provided seems to have been frock coats and pants of jean, with grey forage caps. The former usually had either eight- or nine-button fronts, and collars and cuffs faced with either dark blue or black. Private L. Yates of Co. B, 18th Arkansas Infantry, mustered into Confederate service on 12 March 1862 in an eight-button version of this garment. During the same month, two members of the 23rd Arkansas Infantry were photographed wearing nine-button coats. An officers' version of this uniform, with two rows of five buttons, collar and cuffs faced black, or other branch service colour, and three small buttons on cuff front, may also have existed.

Regarding mounted units, a tinted image of Mark Noble, a trooper in the 2nd Arkansas Cavalry, raised during February 1862 under Colonel Charles W. Phifer, indicates that he wore a nine-button grey frock coat with black collar and plain sleeves; light blue trousers; and a black hat pinned up on the left, with a large black plume held by a yellow metal pin or socket. His shoulder and waist belts were white leather. This may represent an early war uniform, as many members of this regiment were originally part of Phifer's Battalion of Cavalry.

Later in the war, this state uniform issuance largely changed to shell jackets and felt hats. A description of the brigade commanded by General St. John R. Liddell (Cleburne's division of Hardee's corps, Army of Tennessee), which consisted of the 2nd, 5th, 6th, 7th, and 8th Arkansas Infantry regiments, were described in June 1863 as being 'well clothed, though without any attempt at uniformity in color or cut, but nearly all were dressed either in gray or brown coats and felt hats ... many of the soldiers had taken off their coats and marched past the general in their shirt sleeves.'

Photographic evidence indicates that various styles of jackets and coats were issued to Arkansas troops during the second year of the war, and it is difficult to ascertain whether these garments were of state, or C.S. Quartermaster, provenance. Private Francis Warford was issued a grey sack coat with four bone buttons, and open pocket on the left breast, sometime after his enlistment in the 19th Arkansas Infantry on 1 March 1862. Second Lieutenant William W. Crump wore a plain, tight-fitting grey coat devoid of rank insignia, with single row of eight small gilt buttons, sometime after beginning his service with Co. D, 27th Arkansas Infantry, in February 1862. Private Steven K. Porter enlisted in Co. C, 1st Arkansas Cavalry, raised and commanded by Colonel Archibald S. Dobbin in July 1863, wearing a light grey pullover shirt. In a late war image taken in Mobile, Alabama, Joseph V. Bogy, of the Appeal Battery, Arkansas Light Artillery, wore a long grey frock coat with two rows of seven wooden buttons, plain grey pants, grey forage cap with dark, possibly red, band, and gilt crossed cannon insignia on the front.

An unidentified major from Arkansas. Note the revolver pushed into his civilian waistcoat. General Sweeny's Museum, Republic, Missouri.

Tennessee

The uniform regulations in force for Volunteer companies in Tennessee on the eve of the Civil War were based on the 'Militia Laws' of 1840. That for 'Generals and general staff' was to be: 'of the same grade as in the United States army.' Light infantry were to wear: 'long blue hunting shirts, blue pantaloons, round black hat and red plumes'; Riflemen: 'long black hunting shirts, black pantaloons, hats as infantry, and white plumes'; Cavalry: 'Each

Captain Alexander E. Patton, Co. A, 1st Tennessee Infantry (Turney's), initially wore a dark shirt with polka-dotted band sewn down the front, over which was slung a broad webbing-type shoulder belt. Stephen E. Lister.

regiment of cavalry may choose the quality of the uniform for their officers and privates, and they are authorized to use domestic manufactures for the same: Provided, nevertheless, that the coats and pantaloons of each officer and private ... shall be of a deep blue color.' This law also stated that it was permissible for a 'company to choose its own uniform and uniform themselves.' Hence a wide variety of military dress was evident within the state.

The militia system these regulations applied to consisted theoretically of four 'divisions' embracing about 160 'regiments' which were scattered throughout the state. A small number of companies of Volunteer Militia were attached to those regiments located in the regions of Nashville and Memphis. By July 1858, those in Memphis had formed into a battalion which, on 22 March 1860, was organised under Colonel W. H. Carroll into the 154th Regiment of Tennessee Volunteers, using a number in the old militia series. The companies in this regiment included the Memphis Light Guard, the Bluff City Grays, the Jackson Guards, the Harris Zouave Cadets, the Hickory Rifles, the Henry Guards, the Beauregards, the Crockett Rangers, the McNairy Guards, and the Sons of Liberty. Of these, the Harris Zouave Cadets is the most interesting. Originally to be called the Harris Cadets, in honour of Governor Isham G. Harris, this company was organised in June 1860, under the command of Captain C. Sherwin. By August, their name had been changed to the Harris Zouave Cadets, or Memphis Zouaves, having clearly been influenced by the drill tour of Ellsworth's Zouave Cadets that year. Later the same month, they were reported to be wearing 'the Zouave "fatigue" dress consisting of flowing pants with a scarlet stripe, blue roundabout, bound with the same color and plain blue cap.' During a 'Secession Demonstration' which took place by torch-light on the night of 8 February 1861, they paraded 'dressed in their gorgeous scarlet costumes', which suggests they may also have adopted a full zouave uniform.

Another company worthy of note being formed in Memphis during this period was the Highland Guard, raised among the 'Scotch' citizens, who were to be dressed in 'the picturesque uniform of the Highlands of Scotland, plaid, kilt and trews.' It is not known whether the Garibaldi Guards, recruited amongst the Italian population of the city ever adopted a distinctive uniform.

In Nashville a Volunteer Battalion of three companies evolved out of the Rock City Guard, a unit formed in 1860 and named after the ancient nickname of the capital city of Tennessee.

The people of the state were seriously divided in their views on secession from the Union during the early months of 1861. Nonetheless, Governor Harris held extreme pro-slavery tendencies and was in close liaison with Southern leaders. In the wake of success which accompanied the first wave of 'secession fever' to sweep the South, the legislature of the 'Volunteer State' was sufficiently impressed, and determined to entered into a military league with the Confederacy on 6 May 1861. At the same time an act was passed 'to raise, organize and equip a provisional force' to consist of 25,000 men with 30,000 in reserve.

The 'Regulations adopted for the provisional force of the Tennessee volunteers', which accompanied this act, were based on the U.S. regulations of 1857/8. Accordingly, infantry wore dark blue frock coats with sky blue edging. The number of the regiment was worn on the collar. Cavalry, dragoons and mounted rifles wore jackets. Artillery, infantry, mounted rifles and dragoons wore dress caps. Cavalry wore hats. All branches of service wore sky blue pants.

At the same time, 'A Digest of the Militia Laws of Tennessee' stated: 'Tennessee having separated herself from the Federal Union, of course the officers will discontinue that uniform.'

Even before these events, Harris had commenced to raise a state army. The first unit to be formed was the 1st Tennessee Volunteer Infantry (also known as the 1st Confederate Infantry), hastily recruited in the mountain counties of the Middle Tennessee by Colonel Peter Turney. Fully organised by 21 April 1861, this regiment went straight into Confederate service, and was encamped in Virginia by 5 May. Most of the companies of Turney's First marched off to war in their civilian clothes and were uniformed in the vicinity of Richmond by the Confederate government. The Tullahoma Guards, Co. I, acquired distinctive blue caps with long bills. Once these troops had arrived in Virginia, the central government presumably placed orders with local clothiers for

Private Jeter, 8th Tennessee Infantry, wore civilian clothing for this early war image. Stephen E. Lister.

uniforms.

Possibly adopting a very liberal interpretation of the antiquated Tennessee state militia uniform regulations, two officers of the Boon's Creek Minute Men, Co. K, - Captain Newton C. Davis and Lieutenant T. J. Sugg - were subsequently photographed wearing nine-button dark blue, cassimere frock coats, and trousers of the same cloth with broad light-coloured seam stripes. Rank was indicated by Federal-style shoulder straps and waist sashes. Captain Davis wore a Hardee hat looped up on the left after Federal regulations for infantry, whilst Lieutenant Sugg wore a dark blue forage cap with light-coloured band, which may have represented part of the fatigue dress of this company.

A similar, if not identical, style of officers' uniform was in use in regiments including the 11th, 12th, and 16th Tennessee Infantry, during June 1861. This consisted of a dark blue frock coat with light-coloured trim around the bottom of the collar only, plain sleeves, and collar rank consisting of stars and bars, based on Confederate States regulations unofficially published in the New Orleans press in May 1861.

Two unidentified Tennessee infantrymen were photographed by C. Rees of Richmond wearing seven-button grey frock coats with collars and shoulder straps edged with dark-coloured trim. Trousers were also grey with black seam stripes. Another unidentified member of the Fayetteville Guard, Co. G, wore a nine-button grey shell jacket with black facing on collar and cuffs; grey pants with narrow light-coloured seam stripes; and a grey forage cap with black band bearing the brass letters 'FG' in front. The latter may represent later war quartermaster issue.

Other early war units included the Rock City Guard, who wore a chasseur-style uniform consisting of red caps, red flannel trousers and brass buttoned blue coats in January 1861. Expanded to a battalion of three companies by April, they joined the ranks of the 1st Tennessee Infantry (Maney's) wearing a service uniform consisting of a nine-button grey shell jacket with light-coloured facing on collar and cuffs; light grey, or pale blue pants, with dark seam stripes; and forage caps bearing company letters 'A', 'B' and 'C' in front. Sam Watkins of the Maury Grays, Co. H, wore a grey frock coat with dark blue collar, five small buttons on slash sleeves, and black broad-brimmed hat bearing the letter 'H'. Another member of this company wore the same uniform, with a white feather

plume in his hat.

The 3rd Tennessee Infantry, under Colonel John C. Brown, was organised at Lynnville on 16 May, and mustered into Confederate service on 7 August 1861. Private James F. Walker of Company D wore a grey fatigue shirt with light-coloured facing edged with black on buttoned front, cuffs and probably collar. His tall-crowned forage cap quartered with yellow piping was in exactly the same style as that worn by members of the Bate's 2nd Tennessee Infantry. Private John W. McCown of Company C, 3rd (Memphis) Tennessee Battalion, wore a light grey fatigue shirt with turned down collar, pants of the same material with broad dark seam stripes, and grey cap with dark band. John

Johnston recalled receiving 'a gray flannel shirt, gray pants with a dark stripe down each leg and gray coats', when he enlisted in The Danes, Co. K, 6th Tennessee Infantry. The Jackson Grays, of the same regiment, wore a grey coat with black collar, and gray cap with company letter 'G' on its dark band.

Prior to the war, the 1st Company, Tennessee Artillery Corps, commanded by Captain Arthur M. Rutledge, wore blue frock coat, pants and forage cap, with havelock. During May 1861, this unit changed to a short grey coat, grey pants with red seam stripes, and grey felt hat with brass cross cannon inignia. Sergeant Burr Bannister of the 2nd Tennessee Field Battery, commanded by Captain Thomas K. Porter, wore a dark blue M1847 forage cap with light band, and grey frock coat with solid red collar.

Many of the uniforms worn by these early war troops were supplied by the Military and Financial Board of the State of Tennessee, which had been established by 6 May 1861. This Board was composed of three businessmen: Nashville attorney and former Governor, Neil S. Brown; influential owner of Belle Meade plantation, William Giles Harding; and Clarksville attorney, James E. Bailey. At the beginning of May, regimental commanders were instructed to 'draw from the military store cloth, lining, trimmings, buttons & thread for uniforming.' Assistant Quartermaster General E. Foster Cheatham was given a six-step set of instructions outlining how to purchase the cloth, turn it over to contractors, specify the sizes to be made, and deliver the packaged uniforms to the captains of companies.

Some of the first cloth acquired was 'blue jeanes'. Other types available on a commercial basis included 'Cadet Grey Satinets, Blue Satinets, Grey Wool Tweeds, Grey Wool Flannels'. Irby, Morgan & Co., of Nashville, advertised: 'Grey Wool Overshirts' throughout the South. In Memphis, Southworth, Nance & Co., on Main Street, stocked 'Gray and Cadet Cassimeres and Jeans [and] Army Blue Broadcloths'. Among other things, Strauss, Lehman & Co., supplied 'Jeans Pants, Check & Hickory Shirts, Gold Lace and Trimmings, [and] Drab Hats'. Miller & Dunn sold black, brown, gray, and pearl 'wide brim hats'. The 'Southern Cap Manufactory' owned by J. D. Blumenthal, guaranteed that military companies would be 'furnished with any style of Caps desired'. Francisco & Co., were making 'the Zouave Military Cap' by the end of May 1861.

Much of the cloth supplied to the Military and Financial Board was made by the womenfolk of Tennessee. On 8 August 1861, a notice was published in all the newspapers of the state appealing to 'the

Private Hershel Bell Wilson, Co. G, 23rd Tennessee Infantry (left) & Captain Samuel B. Wilson, Co. A, 45th Tennessee Infantry (right). Captain Wilson's dark blue uniform is based on the Tennessee state militia uniform regulations, which in turn were loosely based on those of the U.S. Army as prescribed in 1840. Private Wilson's shoulder and waist belts are of white webbing. His cap pouch is of the type manufactured at the Baton Rouge Arsenal, in New Orleans, whilst he holds a M1842 Musket in the 'Shoulder Arms' position. USAMHI/photo by Jim Enos.

wives, mothers & daughters of Tennessee to manufacture woolen goods & stockings for those who are defending their homes....' It was suggested that 'each lady ... shall prepare goods for one suit of clothing & knit two pairs of stockings. If this shall be done, every soldier will be amply clothed & provided against the suffering of a winter campaign.' Organisations like the 'South Memphis Ladies' Sewing Society' not only provided cloth for the Board, but made up uniforms for the military companies of the city.

Several men from different Tennessee regiments were photographed during the second year of the war wearing remarkably similar uniforms, which suggests a common source of state supply. A hand-tinted image of Private Robert Patterson of Company

F, 55th Tennessee Infantry, a unit raised in February 1862 and commanded originally by Colonel Alexander J. Brown, shows a nine-button dark blue/grey frock coat, and pants, with light blue solid collar and cuffs. Presumably before he became an adjutant of the same regiment, Robert B. Hurt, Jr., was photographed wearing a seven-button coat of the same shade, collar and cuff facings. Also, Private John W. Branch, Co. D, 12th Tennessee Infantry, a regiment reorganised in 1862, wore a coat of exactly the same pattern as Patterson. Towards the end of that year, Tennessee troops began to receive some clothing via the Confederate quartermaster department.

Private James B. Nelson, Madison Invincibles, Co. C, 6th Tennessee Infantry, wears a five-button gray wool shell jacket and cotton jean cloth pants. Clearly visible are his Federal eagle belt plate and Confederate block 'I' infantry buttons.

David Wynn Vaughan collection.

The Stonewall Brigade at First Manassas, 1861.

The 1st Brigade of the Army of the Shenandoah, commanded by Brigadier-General Thomas J. Jackson, earned their legendary nickname at First Manassas on 21 July 1861. Arriving on the battlefield in time to stem the Federal tide sweeping back the Confederate left flank, they gained immortality when General Barnard E. Bee declared: 'Look at Jackson's Brigade! It stands there like a stone wall!'

Liberty Hall Volunteers, Co. I, 4th Virginia Infantry (left) were largely composed of students at Washington College in Lexington. They wore collarless light blue-grey hunting shirts with dark blue trim, on top of white cotton shirts with collars showing; light grey trousers with one inch-wide dark blue seam stripes; and plain blue forage caps with black leather chin strap and visor. Waist belts appear to have been non-regulation and probably home-made, with various buckle styles. They were armed with the U.S. Model 1822 Musket, .69 cal. originally a flintlock but altered to percussion by the thousands between 1843 and 1861. This ungainly weapon weighed more than 10 pounds and measured 57 inches long. Members of this company also provided themselves with short bowie knives.

Marion Rifles, Co. A, 5th Virginia Infantry (centre). Raised in Frederick County, Virginia, this company adopted a nine-button grey frock coat with solid black collar, and three horizontal bands of black braid around the slashed cuffs, which were fastened by three small buttons. Trousers were also grey with black seam stripes. Headgear consisted of plain black felt hats with narrow brim. The figure in the plate wears his pinned up on both sides. His white webbing waist belt supports a black leather cap pouch made at the Baton Rouge Arsenal. He is also armed with a M1822 altered musket.

West Augusta Guard, Co. L, 5th Virginia Infantry (right). Organised at Staunton in the Shenandoah Valley in 1858, the West Augusta Guard, nick-named the 'Wags', wore a version of the state regulation uniform adopted during the same year. This consisted of a dark blue frock coat cut after U.S. regulation pattern and fastened with nine gilt buttons bearing the Virginia State Seal. Collar and cuffs were edged with sky blue piping. Brass shoulder scales were worn for full dress, but these would obviously have been removed for campaign duty, revealing the cloth loop and brass staple by which means they could be attached. Trousers were also dark blue with sky blue seam stripes. 'Hardee' hats followed M1858 U.S. regulation - with yellow metal bugle insignia in front. The brim was looped up on the left by a brass 'eagle' device, with a sky blue worsted hat cord and tassels, and single black ostrich feather attached to the right side of the crown. Their ostrich feather was probably not worn at first Manassas, as members of the Potomac Guards, Co. A, 33rd Virginia Infantry, of the 'Stonewall' Brigade, reported removing theirs on the eve of battle because they believed that the 'Yankees' wore the same.

Painting by Richard Hook.

Private Samuel H. Dunscomb, Co. E, 3rd Battalion Tennessee Infantry, also known as the Memphis Battalion. The letters 'WR' on his hat may indicate that he was a a member of the Washington Rifles, a well established volunteer militia company in Memphis, when this tintype was taken. David Wynn Vaughan collection.

First Sergeant Elbert Monroe Snipes, 37th Tennessee Infantry. His neck tie almost obscures the solid facing on his collar. Dan Snipes, descendant.

These two Tennesseans wear similar uniforms. Joshua T. Martin (left), Company B, 51st Tennessee Infantry (Cheatham's Brigade), fought at Shiloh, and was later discharged at Murfreesboro. Thomas H. Cox (right) was possibly a member of Company I, 45th Tennessee Infantry. Stephen E. Lister/General Sweeny's Museum, Republic.

Below, a M1847 forage cap worn by an officer in the Hardeman Avengers, Co. B, 6th Battalion Tennessee Cavalry. From a photograph by Ron Field.

North Carolina

The first troops to enter active duty from the 'Old North State' were ten uniformed volunteer companies organised for six months service on 13 May 1861 into the 1st Regiment North Carolina Infantry. This regiment went on to take part in the first large-scale land battle of the Civil War, which took place at Big

The Confederate Grays, or Duplin Grays, a volunteer company from Duplin County, parade in camp at Smithville in May or June 1861. Note the shoulder straps on the officers' frock coats, as specified by North Carolina's 1861 uniform regulations. Enlisted men wear seven-button shell jackets with black braid on their pointed cuffs. North Carolina Division of Archives and History.

Bethel on 10 June 1861. The companies which made up this command were some of the oldest in the state. They arrived at the capital wearing their ante-bellum uniforms, probably combined with elements of service dress. Sometime prior to the conflict, Second Lieutenant William S. Long of the Edgecombe Guards, was photographed wearing a dark blue frock coat with a lighter facing colour on collar, epaulette keeps, and cuffs. His slash sleeves were ornamented with eight buttons each. Rank was indicated by gold lace collar loops, and brass epaulettes with narrow gold-bullion fringe. His trousers were also dark blue with broad light-coloured seam stripes. Presumably the NCOs and enlisted men of this company wore a similar

The Iredell Blues, a volunteer militia company, parade in their full dress uniforms, with white summer pants, in front of Stockton Hall in Statesville, ca. 1860. Note the feather plumes fastened to their Mexican War-style caps, and tail coats. Most carry muskets with bayonets, but six men on the left next to the musicians have carbine-like weapons with shortened forestocks. North Carolina Division of Archives and History.

uniform with facing colour appropriate to their rank.

Captain Egbert A. Ross, commanding the Charlotte Grays, of Mecklenburg County, wore a grey pullover shirt with full sleeves, narrow cuffs, and dark facing colour on turned down collar and buttoned front. Rank was indicated by Federal-style shoulder straps sewn to the shoulders of his shirt. His pants were also grey with black seam stripes edged with gold. Ross probably wore this uniform at the head of his company at Big Bethel.

John Thomas Jones, of the Orange Light Infantry, was twice photographed wearing a single-breasted nine-button grey frock coat with dark piping on collar and pointed cuffs. The collar was also decorated with a dark lace loop terminating in a single small button. The cuff had a small button sewn at its point. His headgear consisted of a Model 1839 U.S. forage cap with light-coloured band, and the letters 'OLI' on the front. He wore plain white cotton summer pants.

The Buncombe Rifles were organised at Asheville during December 1859. According to the Charleston *Daily Courier* of 9 January 1860, this company adopted a 'uniform of steel-mixed Rock Island cassimere, made in Mecklenburg County.' Sometime prior to the war, the unit commander, Captain William W. McDowell, was photographed wearing his full dress uniform, which consisted of a single-breasted, seven-button dark steel-grey, frock coat with collar and cuffs edged with light-coloured lace, and double row of piping down front edge and around coat skirts. Rank was indicated by epaulettes and four chevrons on each upper sleeve. His trousers were the same colour,

trimmed with broad light-coloured seam stripes. Headgear consisted of a tall-crowned black hat pinned up on the left with a star insignia, while the front bore the letters 'BR' set within a metal wreath. The uniform for enlisted men seems to have been much simpler, and consisted of a single-breasted, seven button plain, steel-grey frock coat with three large buttons sewn at wide intervals vertically on the front

Second Lieutenant Charles Betts Cook wears the dark blue full dress uniform of the Fayetteville Independent Light Infantry. One of the oldest volunteer militia companies in North Carolina, it became Company H, 1st Regiment N.C. Volunteers in 1861. North Carolina Division of Archives and History.

John V. Jordan, of Craven County, was a major or lieutenant colonel in a militia regiment prior to the war. He was later appointed colonel of the 31st Regiment North Carolina Troops, and surrendered with most of his regiment at Roanoke Island on 8 February 1862. USAMHI/photo by Jim Enos.

First Lieutenant Quentin Busbee, of the Raleigh Rifles, wears a sturdy grey frock coat with shoulder straps. His dark blue forage cap bears the brass characters '4/K/N/C/V' (in mirror image), indicating that his unit became Company K, 4th Regiment N.C. Volunteers. North Carolina Division of Archives and History.

of each sleeve. Coat skirts may have had a broad band of trim, similar in style to many South Carolina companies.

According to an image of an unidentified officer, the LaFayette Light Infantry wore dark blue frock coats, light blue trousers, and Model 1851 dress caps with tall feather plume, before the war. Doubtless, a service dress would have replaced much of this by 1861.

The Enfield Rifles, of Halifax County, wore 'shiny-visored' forage caps, and a 'bright blue tunic' with light-coloured trim around collar and on epaulette keeps. Pantaloons were the same colour. The Southern Stars, who hastily changed their name from Lincoln Guards, in 1861, volunteered in nine-button grey frock coats. One member, and possibly the whole company, wore a large five-pointed star embroidered on his left breast. Their slouch hats were also decorated with a star-shaped brass pin.

Other volunteer militia companies called into service during the first weeks of conflict included the Thomasville Rifles, who later became Co. B, 14th Regiment North Carolina Troops (4th Regiment N.C. Volunteers). Formed in 1859, they adopted Hardee hats with stamped brass bugle horn insignia for riflemen, and dark blue frock coats and pants probably faced with green collar, cuffs and epaulettes. This company appears to have quickly acquired a new issue of grey coats faced green after the beginning of the war. The Guilford Grays, organised in Greensboro during 1860, wore a 'frock coat, single-breasted ... pants to match, with black stripe, waist belt of black leather.'

With little knowledge of the regulations prescribed by the Confederate Government, many of the newly forming companies in North Carolina adopted uniforms of their own choice. The Moore's Creek Rifle Guards acquired light blue forage caps, and dark blue nine-button frock coats with red cuffs. The

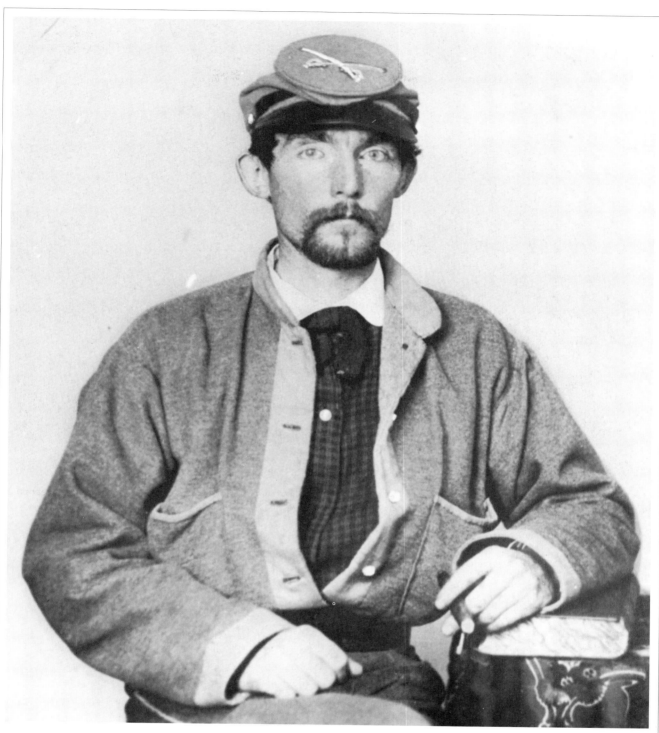

Mountain Tigers volunteered in six-button plain grey frock coats, with very large outside pockets on their right breasts. The Caldwell Rough and Ready Boys chose plain, possibly red, overshirts and light-coloured kepis. The Poplar Spring Grays wore very substantial seven-button grey frock coats with light-coloured edging around collar, cuffs, and across their shoulders. The Montgomery Grays adopted nine-button grey frock coats with bars of dark tape-trim across their chests.

One of the most reputable sources for cloth in North Carolina and, indeed, throughout the South

John Lawson Wrenn, may be the same man as the 'John A. Wren' who served as a private in the Buncombe Rangers, Co. G, 1st Regiment N.C. Cavalry. His unusual shell jacket, worn over a checkered civilian shirt, may be trimmed yellow in branch service colour. Likewise his pants. He clearly enjoyed a cigar. North Carolina Division of Archives and History.

during the years before the war, was the Rock Island Manufacturing Company of Charlotte, in Mecklenburg County. Run by Young & Wriston, they produced 'a very superior article of goods for uniforms', and their 'Cassimeres' won several awards at

William Rhem enlisted in Guion's Battery, Co. B, 10th Regiment N.C. Troops (1st Regiment N.C. Artillery), on 23 July 1861. He is clad in grey forage cap and light grey overshirt. The dark trim on collar, cuffs, and front seam may be red. The small letters and/or numerals on his cap top are too indistinct to read. *North Carolina Division of Archives and History.*

Private William C. Steele, Company D, 33rd Regiment, N.C. Troops, wears the six-button grey sack with sewn-down black epaulettes specified in uniform regulations issued by the North Carolina adjutant general in 1861. His cap appears to be dark blue. Accoutrements are black leather, whilst his hand rests on a tin drum canteen. *North Carolina Division of Archives and History.*

State Fairs during 1860. Other antebellum firms producing 'yarn and cotton osnaburgs' included the Eagle Mills, owned by Messrs. Colvert & Co.; and the mills owned by W. Turner, at Turnersburg - both situated in Iredell County. Cotton factories were also operating in Yadkin, Surry, Catawba, Cumberland and elsewhere.

Troops organising for war in 1861 found a great variety of clothing available for purchase in cities such as Raleigh and Wilmington. E. L. Harding, in the capital, advertised 'Military Goods just received from Richmond, Virginia', which included 'Grey Flannel shirts for soldiers.' These were also available in red, 'Checked Gingham', and 'Mixed Cassimere.' O. S. Baldwin, of Wilmington, advised that he was 'Contracting for Making and Trimming Uniforms', for those companies with their own cloth.

An anonymous letter to the editor of the Raleigh *North Carolina Standard*, published on 1 May 1861,

urged the units organising for war to buy uniforms of North Carolina grey cassimere. 'Its advantages', it was argued, were that it '...is cheap, that it will last well, and the experiments made by the French Emperor prove that grey is the most difficult color to take sight upon, hence is less often hit. Again, it is the product of our own soil. I have lately seen a company uniformed in blue broadcloth and Northern blue cassimere. Now, that is just the uniform of the regular U.S. troops, further it is of northern make and very expensive. If a man expects to go into service there is no sense in his wearing his ball-room clothes, no more than there is in his going into a pig-pen with them.'

The first attempt by state authorities to regulate the clothing of its military forces was partial and makeshift. In a general order of 20 April 1861, Adjutant General John F. Hoke directed that volunteers were to wear 'blue or gray blouses.' A much more substantial effort was made on 23 May, when

Governor John W. Ellis appointed a board of officers to determine a uniform for the new regiments of State Troops and volunteers being rapidly formed. Their findings were formalised in General Orders No. 1 on 27 May, which created a uniform which hereafter will be called the state 1861 pattern. In its several varieties, this uniform was worn by most of North Carolina's soldiers thoughout the remainder of the conflict. Details of it were prescribed by published regulations, printed shortly after at the 'N.C. Inst. for the Deaf & Dumb & the Blind.' Essentially, these regulations called for dark blue frock coats and trousers for general officers and staff, the same in grey for regimental officers, and grey sack coats and pantaloons 'of North Carolina Manufacture' for all enlisted men, with branch of service colours of buff, red, yellow and black for general officers and staff, artillery, cavalry and infantry respectively.

In anticipation of this move, a notice appeared in the newspapers, dated 18 May, advising that: 'Tailors and others wishing to contract for making Uniform Clothing for the North Carolina Troops are requested to make immediate application at the Quarter Master's General's Office in Raleigh. The material will be delivered to the contractors at any railroad depot in the state.' The distinctive enlisted men's six-button sack coat, with falling collar and shoulder trim, produced via this source, was provided by the state to a considerable number of companies that decided to purchase it with their commutation money, rather than fending for themselves.

By September 1861 the current stocks of state uniforms were exhausted, and it became very apparent that the Confederate government would be unable to provide clothing before the winter. Hence, on 21st of that month the legislature reorganised the military departments, which resulted in the hasty establishment of a clothing manufactory at Raleigh under Captain I. W. Garrett. Every mill in the state was urged to furnish every possible yard of cloth, whilst further contracts were let for caps, shoes and accoutrements. Agents were also sent into several other Southern states to purchase everything that could be used for clothing.

On 10 February 1862, Assistant Quartermaster Major John Deveraux wrote to a firm with which the state had contracts, 'I will be obliged ... if you will cut no more coats but cut all jackets, a sample will be sent you in a few days.' Hence the sack coat was modified by removing the skirts and turning it into a six-button jacket. The falling collar and shoulder trim were retained on this garment. The next stage in the modification of the state jacket occurred during the

This unidentified 'Tar Heel' wears the state regulation grey cap, trousers, and sack coat with black epaulettes. He is armed with a M1842 U.S. musket, a holstered revolver (possibly the Colt M1849 revolver) and has what appears to be a Smith and Wesson 'Model No. 1' rimfire revolver, calibre .22, pushed into his belt. His waist belt is secured by a rectangular brass plate, and supports a cap pouch under his arm. He also carries a tin drum canteen, and black rubberised cloth haversack. North Carolina Division of Archives and History.

summer of 1862 with the elimination of the coloured shoulder trim and the replacement of the falling collar

Andrew Jackson Daniel, Trio Guards, 61st Regiment N.C. Troops, wears a seven-button version of the 'second pattern' jacket issued by the state during 1862. He is accoutered with a waist belt secured by a roller buckle, and a cartridge box and sling. He holds a Pattern 1853 Enfield rifle-musket, calibre .577. North Carolina Division of Archives and History.

Jacob Calvin Williams was elected second lieutenant of the Auburn Guards, Co. C, 31st Regiment N.C. Troops, on 4 October 1862. His grey frock with shoulder straps probably dates from soon after his promotion. His Hardee hat is adorned with a metal star insignia and black ostrich feather. North Carolina Division of Archives and History.

by a more orthodox standing collar, making a 'second pattern' plain six-button jacket. This type was issued till the end of the war. Thus, between 30 September 1861 and 30 September 1862 Garrett had manufactured for the Quartermaster's Department, the following: '5,979 overcoats, 49,093 jackets, 5,954 coats, 68,364 pants, 61,275 shirts ...'

Regarding headgear, General Officers and Staff were originally prescribed black felt hats, whilst Commissioned Officers and other ranks were to acquire grey felt hats, with branch of service insignia. Also, forage caps were to be worn by all ranks 'when off duty or on fatigue duty.' Those for officers were to be of the 'French'-pattern, whilst enlisted men's were 'grey'. During the year ending 30 September 1862 slightly fewer than 9,000 hats were issued, compared with 60,000 caps. Supply problems inevitably affected the type and colour of both hats and caps available. Some blue caps were supplied via Marshall Parks,

North Carolina's purchasing agent in Norfolk, Virginia, under the state's first cap contract. On 1 June 1861, Quartermaster General Lawrence O'Bryan Branch wrote to Parks: 'If gray can be had, please require the maker to furnish only that color. I will not object to different shades of gray, provided they are packed in different cases so that my assts. can put an entire Regiment in the same shade.' Whatever the colour, Parks acquired the caps from W. H. C. Lovitt, of Virginia. Some brown caps may have been issued in early 1862, since Devereaux wrote to a supplier on 17 January, instructing him to 'cut no more caps out of the brown kerseys sent you. Genl. Martin objects to a variegated color.' While infantry were supplied with grey caps with black bands, and plain grey caps, red and yellow bands were put on the caps supplied, probably, to the 1st Artillery and Second Cavalry, judging by Devereaux's instructions to another contractor in December 1861 to 'bind 1000 caps with

red for artillery', and, in February 1862, to send '1000 caps bound with yellow for cavalry.'

When in October 1862 the Confederate government abandoned the commutation system, and took over the responsibility for clothing the state troops in her service, North Carolina insisted, in a fine display of state's rights defiance, on continuing to furnish her own, taking payment for supplies turned over by her to the Confederate quartermaster to issue to North Carolina troops. With the approach of another winter of war, the situation was becoming critical. Short term measures saw the state troops through the worst, but

The Cathey brothers, of Jackson County, served in the Jackson Rangers, or Jackson Volunteers, a unit which became Company A, 6th Regiment N.C. Troops. All three brothers, and possibly the whole company, wore light-coloured slouch hats with their state uniforms. Benjamin Hamilton Cathey stands with his musket at 'Support Arms' at centre. William Hillman Cathey also holds a small pocket revolver at left. Francis Marion Cathey sits at right. North Carolina Division of Archives and History.

as a long-term solution, the state turned to blockade-running. Agent John White was mainly responsible for purchases in England, principally through middlemen Alexander Collie & Co. Initially White was instructed to buy '400,000 yards woollen cloth for soldiers' uniforms, 25,000 yards gray cloth for officers' uniforms, 150,000 yards blue flannel for shirts, 60,000 pairs shoes...'

From June 1863, when the first shipment arrived, to January 1865, when Fort Fisher fell, North Carolina is believed to have imported, at an approximate total, grey wool cloth sufficient for 250,000 suits of uniforms, and 12,000 overcoats; 50,000 blankets; and leather and shoes for 250,000 pairs. The cloth imported is believed to have been a dark bluish-grey shade which was quite distinct from the drab greys of the Confederate-made jeans cloth of the period, and is sometimes referred to as 'blue', or 'English blue'. In a much-quoted recollection Governor Zebulon B. Vance later estimated that the state had on hand '92,000 suits of uniforms' at the war's end.

This is the only known image of a mounted North Carolina cavalryman. Captain John W. Woodfin of the Buncombe Rangers, Co. G, 1st Regiment N.C. Cavalry, sits astride his black charger 'Prince Hal'. Woodfin wears a single-breasted grey frock coat, and grey pants with a yellow seam stripe. He has a dark blue forage cap, and his armed with a cavalry sabre. North Carolina Division of Archives and History.

Missouri

On the eve of the Civil War, the old enrolled militia system of Missouri had been all but abandoned, and the state's sole military force consisted of uniformed Volunteer Militia companies, the majority of which resided in St. Louis and Jefferson City, the state capital. An act of state legislature passed in 1859 authorised these companies, some of which were organised into regiments and battalions along the lines of the defunct enrolled militia, to choose their own uniforms, and for general officers to do likewise. The dress chosen by some of these companies may have been influenced by the uniforms of their grandfathers,

as prescribed by the state legislature on 22 June 1821, which called for: 'Officers in —Blue hunting shirts trimmed with red, white pantaloons and vest, black hat with a black cockade and red plume—noncoms to be uniformed as above, except hunting shirts trimmed with white, [and] white plumes—.'

The slavery issue, and the Kansas/Missouri Border War of 1856, had already sharply divided the state, but when Governor Claiborne F. Jackson, a strong Southern sympathiser, was inaugurated in 1861, he made it clear that he intended to stand by the South in the approaching conflict. The military companies which also avowed that cause tended to be of older American, or Irish, stock and filled the ranks of the 1st Missouri Brigade, Volunteer Militia, based at St. Louis. Generally these companies were distinctively garbed, but regimental uniforms were adopted by several units by 1861. The 1st Missouri Infantry Regiment wore a uniform consisting of blue frock coats, sky blue pants, and M1851 cloth dress cap, based on the State Regulations of 1858, which in turn were largely based on U.S. Army regulations, with the exception of the eagle and wreath cap insignia and white worsted epaulettes, instead of shoulder scales.

The Pioneer Corps attached to this regiment also wore a blue frock coat, trimmed with red and gold lace; dark grey pants with wide red seam stripes; bearskin hats with red bag, cord and tassels, red, white and blue plume; and high black leather boots. They

Emmitt MacDonald was captain of the St. Louis Artillery, a company of the 1st Regiment, Missouri Volunteer Militia, at the beginning of the Civil War. He went on to command the 3rd Battery, Light Artillery, C.S.A., and fought at Wilson's Creek, Lexington and Pea Ridge. He wears a well-lined grey jacket of zouave style, trimmed on collar, cuffs and edges. Note the small, light-coloured trefoil braid underneath the collar. His Model 1851 grey dress cap, with lighter-coloured band, has the cardboard stiffening removed to give the appearance of a fatigue cap. General Sweeny's Museum, Republic, Missouri.

The Duval brothers: Private Thomas Duval (left), and Lieutenant William Duval (right), served originally in the Missouri State Guard, before joining the 3rd Missouri Infantry. They both wear homemade fatigue shirts with light-coloured trimming, reminiscent of the 1821 regulations. Note the secession cockade pinning up Private Duval's hat brim. General Sweeny's Museum, Republic, Missouri.

also wore full beards and carried axes! The Engineer Corps wore blue frock coats edged with yellow lace, with gilt engineer castle insignia on collar and dress cap.

The individual companies within this regiment reserved distinctive uniforms for special occasions. The Emmet Guard wore blue tail coats faced with buff; and sky blue pants with buff seam stripes. The Washington Blues had a similar coat with light blue facings, and dark blue pants with light blue stripes. Both of these companies adopted bearskin caps in 1857. The St. Louis Grays, Co. D of this regiment in 1861, wore a light grey tail coat with sky blue facings and epaulettes; black dress cap; light grey pants with wide blue seam stripe.

The Missouri Light Artillery chose a blue frock coat with red collar and cuffs edged with gold lace; brass shoulder scales; sky blue pants with double red

seam stripes; and a sky blue felt cap with patent leather top, brass flaming shell device, and red horsehair plume hanging on the right side.

Zouave 'fever' began in St. Louis with the visit of the celebrated United States Zouave Cadets on 10 August 1860. Influenced by their drill and showy uniforms, the 2nd Missouri Regiment, a pro-slavery unit organised in the city during February 1861, adopted as a regimental uniform a dark grey zouave jacket and full pants, trimmed with black cord; grey shirt; and grey cap with black top. At least one company of the 1st Regiment, the St. Louis Artillery, may also have worn this, or a similar, zouave uniform.

On 3 May 1861 the 1st and 2nd Regiments, Missouri Volunteer Militia, gathered at Camp Jackson outside St. Louis intent on taking over the U.S. Arsenal in the city. Captured by pro-Unionist forces under Captain Nathaniel Lyon seven days later, they were subsequently demobilised, but many of them made for Memphis, Tennessee, where they formed the 1st Missouri Volunteer Infantry and fought for the Confederacy.

In response to the Federal capture of Camp Jackson, the Confederate government of Governor Jackson, at Jefferson City, passed legislature on 14 May readying the state for defense, and establishing the State Guard, which was to be formed out of the rural elements of the Volunteer Militia. Led by Major General Sterling Price, this force was forced to retire to the southwestern corner of the state. At its height, the State Guard amounted to about 7,000 men formed into some 62 poorly organised battalions, drawn from geographical divisions of the state, each division representing a congressional district. Without uniforms, and in some cases without weapons, they repelled the Union columns sent to destroy them. Captain Otto C. Lademann, of the Union 3rd Infantry, recalled the State Guard at the battle of Carthage, 5 July 1861: 'The enemy had no uniforms being entirely clad in homespun butternut jeans worn by every farmer in those days.' Acting Adjutant General of the Missouri State Guard, Colonel Thomas L. Snead, observed of his comrades: 'In all their motley array there was hardly a uniform to be seen, and then, and throughout all the brilliant campaign on which they were about to enter[,] there was nothing to distinguish their officers, even a general, from the men in the ranks, save a bit of red flannel, or a piece of cotton cloth, fastened to the shoulder, or to the arm, of the former.'

Entries found in an account book for the Missouri State Guard indicate that their Quartermaster must have literally cleaned out every store encountered in

an attempt to supply the troops. When clothing was not available, bolts of cloth were purchased and issued to the men, from which they made their own. One of the more unusual purchases, made on 3 July 1861 of Hyatt & Allen, included '24 Buffalo robes at $4.50'! By 2 December 1861, the Missouri State Guard began to break up, and many of its units were transferred as volunteers into Confederate service, and at various points thereafter were in receipt of clothing from the central government. Other elements of the State Guard joined guerrilla bands which continued to operate in Missouri. The most notable of these was

Private S. W. Stone, California Guards, and Private P. S. Alexander, Moniteau County Rangers, Missouri State Guard. Taken at Jefferson City in May 1861, soon after the formation of the Missouri State Guard, the only sign of possible military dress on these men is the cap worn by Private Stone, who is armed with a musket, and wears a fancy tooled leather holster and double buckle accoutrement belt which also supports a bowie knife. Alexander holds a double-barrel shotgun, and has a wide leather shoulder belt which probably supports a cartridge box. A large knife is stuck in his belt, and a bouquet of wild flowers adorns his hat. General Sweeny's Museum, Republic, Missouri.

that led by William Clarke Quantrill who, in time: '...developed a dress peculiar to themselves which became known up and down the border. Its distinguishing item was a "guerrilla shirt." This shirt, patterned after the hunting coat of the Western plainsmen, was cut low in front, the slit narrowing to a point above the belt and ending in a rossette. The garment had four big pockets, two in the breast, and ranged in color from brilliant red to homespun butternut. They were made by the mothers, wives, and sweethearts of the guerrillas, and many were elaborately decorated with colored needlework.'

Quantrill's Guerrilla's also fought in captured blue Federal uniforms, prompting General Orders No. 100 from the U.S. Adjutant General's office, dated 24 April 1863, which stipulated: 'Troops who fight in the uniform of their enemies, without any plain, striking and uniform mark of distinction of their own, can expect no quarter.'

Henderson Duval, also of the Missouri State Guard, wears a plain civilian shirt tucked into military trousers with light, possibly gold, coloured seam stripe. He appears to be holding a Tucker and Sherrod & Co., .44-calibre revolver, whilst a horse pistol is pushed into the waist band of his pants. General Sweeny's Museum, Republic, Missouri.

Kentucky

With the approach of Civil War, and opinion divided on State's Rights, it became apparent to military experts in Kentucky that the militia system of that state was in need of total reform. Its enrolled militia was defunct, and only a few Volunteer Militia companies existed within its borders. Simon Bolivar Buckner, was a West Pointer of the Class of 1844, who had distinguished himself in the Mexican War. Resigning from the U.S. Army in 1855, he continued his military career as captain of the Citizen's Guard of Louisville. Under instructions from Governor Beriah Magoffin he drew up plans for an entirely new militia system for Kentucky which included the 'State Guard', a corps of uniformed volunteer militia created via act of legislature on 5 March 1860. Subsequently appointed Adjutant General and Commander of this new force, Buckner re-visited West Point to obtain ideas for the uniform to be worn by the state board. After several days of discussion with instructor of artillery Rufus Saxton, a uniform of grey trimmed with black and gold was decided upon - which happened to be the main colours worn by both West Point Cadets, and the Citizen's Guard of Louisville.

It is difficult to ascertain exactly when it was adopted but, by August 1860, Buckner and other officers of the Kentucky State Guard began to appear in the new uniform. Made of cadet grey cloth, generals and field officers wore a double-breasted frock coat, with collar and cuffs faced with black velvet based 1857 U.S. Army regulations. That worn by Buckner survives in the collection of the Museum of the Confederacy. Made from grey wool broadcloth, his general officer's rank insignia consisted of an embroidered silver shield flanked by two five-pointed stars; and a silver eagle on black velvet shoulder straps bordered with two rows of silver lace edged with thin gold cord.

Other Kentuckian general officers photographed in this uniform include George B. Crittenden, Humphrey Marshall, and Benjamin H. Helm,

Abraham Lincoln's brother-in-law. Photographed officers of lesser grade in this uniform indicate that a complicated collar and shoulder strap rank insignia system was in use throughout the short period of existence of the Kentucky State Guard. At some point in early 1861, the general officer's version of this uniform was miscontrued as the regulation dress of the new Confederacy, and convenient photographs were

Simon Bolivar Buckner in the Kentucky State Guard uniform he designed in 1860. Two rows of Kentucky State buttons are arranged in groups of three in line with 1857 U.S. Army regulations for a Major General. His slash cuffs are fastened by three small buttons.

The pleated hunting coat worn by Simon Bolivar Buckner. Cut in a style similar to that worn in South Carolina, it was made of brownish-grey wool and cotton cloth and fastened by Kentucky State buttons. A white wool yarn general's insignia was embroidered on a black wool backing affixed to the turndown collar. The Museum of the Confederacy.

altered to show these distinctive collar and shoulder devices on a variety of persons.

Company-grade officers wore a single-breasted version of this uniform with black cloth collar, cuffs, and shoulder straps. Officers caps of chasseur pattern were cadet grey with a black band quartered by gold lace trim. Trousers were also cadet grey with a light-coloured, possibly gold, seam stripes.

Staff N.C.O.s of the Kentucky State Guard wore a single-breasted coat with plain collar and cuffs, and plain black cotton shoulder straps. Rank insignia consisted of black inverted chevrons. Short brown buttoned gaiters were worn by both officers and men.

According to Buckner's wife, a 'Hunting shirt', in imitation of 'the clothes of the pioneers of the state', was encouraged as a fatigue dress of the Kentucky State Guard. That worn by General Buckner is held today in the collection of the Museum of the Confederacy. The Jefferson Rifles, a volunteer militia

company organised by John Hunt Morgan, wore a similar style of shirt.

With the outbreak of hostilities in 1861, Kentucky adopted a neutral position, and many Kentuckians with southern sympathies made their way to the newly formed Confederate States to offer their services. Colonel Blanton Duncan formed a battalion at Harper's Ferry during April-May 1861, and uniformed them in hunting shirts possibly based on those worn by the Kentucky State Guard. This unit became part of the 1st Kentucky Infantry. Numerous Kentuckians entering Tennessee during June 1861 led to the organisation of the 2nd and 3rd Kentucky Infantry regiments at Camp Boone, Montgomery County. These two units were supplied by the wealthy citizens of Louisville, and many appear to have worn their State Guard uniform. As further regiments were formed in southern Kentucky and northern Tennessee, volunteers provided their own uniforms.

However, by October 1861 a clothing shortage became evident. At Bowling Green, Kentucky, Quartermaster V. K. Stevenson, unable to supply adequate uniforms to Colonel Thomas H. Hunt's 5th Kentucky Infantry, advised that company captains supply only those men in most need. At Clarksville, near Camp Boone, 200 women were put to work making clothing for the 2nd, 3rd and 4th Kentucky Infantry regiments. Meanwhile, at Camp Alcorn, near Hopkinsville, Kentucky, the Quartermaster admitted that he was 'entirely deficient.'

Nonetheless, the lack of heavy campaigning, and large amount of clothing that volunteers brought with them, probably enabled Kentuckians to stay well uniformed into late 1861. Private Thomas W. Blandford, 8th Kentucky Mounted Infantry, wore a double-breasted mid-grey frock coat with two rows of seven Kentucky State buttons, an outside pocket set at an angle level on the left breast, and black collar and pointed cuffs. Held by the Museum of the Confederacy, a small pin is still attached to it, which consists of a dull silver star, with 'KY' engraved on it, attached to which is a crescent engraved with the motto 'Nil Desperandum'. A red silk ribbon, probably the remains of a cockade, hangs from this pin.

In his recollections of service as an officer in the 4th Kentucky Cavalry, George D. Musgrove remarked that as a rule he was: '...fond of gay attire, his style being regulation cavalry boots, a red sash, a large black felt hat, of the slouch variety, with the brim of one side turned up and pinned to the side of the crown with a silver crescent or star, the whole surmounted by a huge, black ostrich plume.'

As the 2nd Kentucky Cavalry, commanded by John

The uniform of the Kentucky State Guard, 1860-61. Brigadier-General (left); Sergeant-Major (centre); Brigadier-General's shoulder strap (right). From photographs and descriptions by Richard Warren.

Hunt Morgan, set out from Knoxville in 1862 on its first major raid, they were described as lacking 'general uniforms', although some were in 'new regulation gray, others in butternut jeans.' Members of Co. E and Co. F were photographed wearing light grey, seven- and eight-button shell jackets with solid, possibly yellow, facings on collar and cuffs. The latter appear to have been slashed and unusually fastened by a row of six small buttons along the back seam. This feature also appears on a plain, nine-button jacket worn by Thomas Bronston Collins, Co. F, 11th Kentucky Cavalry. Eighteen small buttons were sewn on each of Collins' cuffs! Most of these cavalrymen appear to have worn narrow-brimmed black felt hats. That worn by T. B. Collins was looped up on one side by a small, five-pointed metal star.

The 1st Kentucky Brigade (known today as the 'Orphan Brigade' because its members left home to fight for the Confederacy), composed of the 2nd, 3rd,

4th, 6th, and 9th Kentucky Infantry regiments, were in receipt of Confederate quartermaster-issue clothing, probably from the Columbus Depot, from late 1862 until the end of 1864.

Private Henry C. Hally, Co. A, 4th Kentucky Infantry wore this dark cadet grey frock coat with nine Kentucky State buttons, with a mid-blue collar, epaulette keeps, belt tabs, and pointed cuffs. The latter were slash and fastened by two small buttons on the back seams. A thin cord of mid-blue piping also ran down the front fastening edge. Hally may have worn this coat prior to the war as a member of a volunteer militia company. Stones River National Battlefield Park.

Maryland

As a border slave state, Maryland was in a very difficult position at the outbreak of the Civil War. Secessionists both inside and outside her borders had struggled for many years to align her with the South, whilst others sought to keep her in the Union. This divided allegiance was reflected in her Volunteer Militia, particularly in Baltimore, where certain commands such as the 5th and 53rd Infantry Regiments, strongly avowed the Southern cause. Consequently, when

Robert G. Harper wearing the uniform of the Maryland Guard Battalion. He would later serve the Confederacy as a lieutenant on the staff of General Richard Ewell. Dave Mark Collection.

Federal forces under General Benjamin Butler occupied the state capital in April 1861, these militia units were forbidden to assemble, and ceased to function. However, many of its members - singly, in small groups, and on a few occasions even by companies - stole out of Baltimore and made for Virginia. By early May, six companies of Maryland infantry had coalesced at Harpers Ferry and four more in Richmond. Those in the Confederate capital were temporarily designated Weston's Battalion. Nine of these companies would shortly join the ranks of the fledgling Virginia army as the 1st Maryland Infantry.

The tenth company (one of the three at Richmond), under Captain J. Lyle Clarke, and composed of 109 ex-members of the Maryland Guard Battalion, became Co. B, 21st Virginia Infantry and served in the Army of Northern Virginia until May 1862. The uniforms received by Clarke's company were made by the Richmond firm of Kent, Paine and Co. Described as being of 'coarse grey, but very durable', that worn by Private E. Courtney Jenkins survives at the Museum of the Confederacy, and consists of a six-button shell jacket and trousers made of heavy satinette. The six-button jacket collar, shoulder straps, and trouser outer seams, are bound in half-inch black tape. Thin grey tape belt loops are attached near the jacket's side seams. Two of the other Maryland companies in Richmond also appear to have received this type of uniform.

The six Harpers Ferry companies remained ununiformed and poorly clad until they amalgamated with the three from Weston's Battalion at Winchester, Virginia, on 25 June 1861. At this point, Jane Claudia Johnson, wife of the major of the consolidated 1st Maryland Infantry, 'secured cloth ... by purchasing it from the mills where it was manufactered for the State of Virginia, and she paid for making it up into uniforms.' Thus the remaining companies of the 1st Maryland were supplied with uniforms consisting of 'a French kepi (a little gray cap), a *(continued p.114)*

Two corporals of the pre-war Maryland Guard Battalion, a volunteer militia unit organised in 1859. John Eager Howard Post (left) enlisted as a private in the 1st Maryland Infantry and was later commissioned lieutenant in the 1st Maryland Cavalry. Charles R. Thompson (right) served as a private in the same cavalry regiment. Both men wear the full dress ('Class A') chasseur uniform of the Maryland Guard Battalion, which consisted of a dark blue jacket and pantaloons trimmed with yellow; a blue flannel shirt trimmed yellow down the front, and red around the neck; light blue cap with dark blue band, quartered and trimmed with yellow lace; wide red sash; and 'drab' gaiters. The numerals '53' on their rigid militia knapsack denotes the number of the militia regiment to which this battalion was attached. Note the letters 'M' and 'G' just visible on the blue blanket roll. Dave Mark collection.

Opposite
Captain James Thomas Bussey led Co. H, 2nd Maryland Infantry. His double-breasted grey jacket has been created by either cutting the skirts off his frock coat or, more likely, simply tucking them into his pants. Dave Mark Collection.

natty gray roundabout roundabout, collar and sleeves bound with black braid, and a similar stripe down the gray trousers.' This uniform was in all probablity patterned on those made by Kent, Paine and Co. for the three Richmond-based companies earlier in the year. Non-commissioned officers wore their black chevrons point down on their right sleeves only.

A zouave unit was raised in Maryland by Richard Thomas, of St. Mary's County. Born in 1833, Thomas was educated at Charlotte Hall and Oxford, Maryland, and briefly at the U.S. Military Academy. At first as a surveyor and later as a soldier of fortune, he spent years on the western frontier and in fighting river pirates in China. He also fought with Garibaldi in Italy. There he adopted the title and name of 'Colonel Richard Thomas Zarvona', by which he called himself thereafter. An ardent secessionist, he joined with others, including G. W. Alexander and William Walters, to form two infantry companies in St. Mary's and Calvert counties, Maryland, to 'be drilled as Zouaves for the Confederate service.' Members of these companies, led by 'Colonel Zarvona', captured a Chesapeake Bay steamer, the *St. Nicholas*, on 28 June 1861, and went on to take three Federal merchant vessels. At Fredericksburg Confederate authorities honoured the action, and Governor Letcher of Virginia commissioned Zarvona a colonel in the state forces.

Zarvona was subsequently described in the Richmond press as presenting 'a picturesque appear-ance, attired in his blue Zouave costume, white gaiters, red cap with gold tassel and light elegant sword.' A red fez with a dark blue tassel, believed to have belonged to Zarvona, survives today in the collection of the Maryland Historical Society.

By early July 1861, plans were underway to organise the Maryland Zouaves, 1st Regiment, with William Walters in command of the 'first company', and G. W. Alexander as adjutant. Meanwhile, Zarvona became involved in further naval escapades on the Chesapeake Bay, was captured and imprisoned for two years in a Federal prison, and finally freed in April 1863 on the understanding that he would live abroad until the war was over.

The Maryland Zouaves, 1st Regiment, failed to materialise, and the Zouave company led by Walters was designated Co. H, 47th Virginia Infantry. After service on the Peninsula, this unit was transferred to the 2nd Arkansas Battalion, and was mustered out of service on 10 June 1862.

Corporal Francis Higdon, Robertson's Company, 1st Maryland Infantry. Higdon's company received their uniforms in August 1861. His Corsican-style cap with black band is made of the same material as the jacket, and may indicate that the whole of his company received head gear of this type. On the other hand this may have been a personalised item specific to Higdon. Note the corporal's chevrons are on the right sleeve only. USAMHI/Photo by Jim Enos.

Confederate Quartermaster Issue

The bulk of uniforms supplied by the Quartermaster's Department during the Civil War had little to do with the official Confederate dress regulations produced in June 1861, the design of which was possibly based on the Austrian jaeger uniform, generally believed to have been suggested by Nicola Marschall, a German artist who emigrated to the U.S. in 1849. These regulations called for double-breasted frock coats, or tunics, of medium grey with a bluish cast, known as 'cadet gray'. Also specified was a system of branch colour on collar and cuffs, with blue for infantry, red for artillery, yellow for cavalry. Trousers were full cut and sky blue. Forage caps were grey with a band of branch colour. Overcoats were cadet grey, and cut like those issued to the U.S. Army. Officer's rank insignia consisted of bars and stars on the collar, and an 'Austrian knot' on each sleeve.

The tardiness in publication of these regulations, the expensive composition of the uniforms prescribed, and difficulties experienced by the general government in taking over any serious issue of clothing until late 1861, led to very few of these uniforms being produced and worn. However, the 1861 regulations did accomplish several important things. They set the style of dress of the Confederate officer. They

Plate from the Confederate dress regulations of 6 June 1861.
Author's collection.

SERGEANT   PRIVATE   MUSICIAN

An unidentified Confederate enlisted man wearing the uniform coat specified in the Confederate regulations published in June 1861. Michael J. McAfee.

established a branch colour system, and pattern of buttons. Most importantly, they did much to establish grey as the official colour of the upper garment of the Confederate Army, in contrast with the dark blue being specified during the same period by their Northern counterparts. This choice of colour was further influenced by a popular belief in the U.S. that grey uniforms should be worn by volunteers, as opposed to the dark blue of the regular army.

As a result of the commutation system established by the Confederate government in February 1861, volunteers of the Provisional Army were originally to provide their own clothing, for which they would receive $21 every six months. This was supplemented

Opposite
Richmond Depot Jackets. First pattern (top) cadet grey Richmond Bureau jacket. Second pattern (centre) - minus trim. Third pattern (bottom) - minus shoulder straps, which were sometimes used as belt loops.

Private Alexander Murray served in Company A, 2nd Maryland Infantry, and was wounded at Culp's Hill. He wears a Richmond Depot, second pattern shell jacket. Dave Mark Collection.

at Nashville, Tennessee; Montgomery, Tuscaloosa and Marion, Alabama; Jackson and Enterprise, Mississippi; Athens, Atlanta and Columbus, Georgia and elsewhere. By 8 October 1861 the quartermaster issue system was considered to be strong enough to supply the Confederate fighting forces with uniforms directly, and the commutation system was officially ended. This is not to suggest that all Confederate units now began to receive government clothing. Some of the very needy regiments had been on the issue system as early as the summer of 1861. Others did not get on it until late 1862 or early 1863, and had meanwhile to make do with whatever clothing the folks back home could make up for them. Evidence suggests that some troops in the West did not get off the commutation system until 1864. However, the issue system was largely in place and functioning by 1864 within the main Confederate armies.

Part of the full clothing allowance for enlisted men for a three year period of service, established in December 1862, consisted of two jackets in the first year and one a year thereafter. They also received three pairs of trousers in the first year and two per year thereafter. Caps were issued at the rate of two for the first year, and one per year thereafter. It has been estimated that the average Confederate soldier on campaign would wear out a jacket in three months, whilst trousers lasted only a month. Hence, despite what would appear to be a generous clothing allowance, the Confederate army in the field was often in a sorry and ragged state.

The pattern and colour of the uniforms supplied varied from the outset. Despite the fact that 'tunics' were called for in the 1861 regulations, the uniform supplied from 1862 onwards always included the 'roundabout' or 'shell jacket', which was a much cheaper garment to produce than the frock coat or tunic. Although no quartermaster department examples survive, photographic evidence suggests that the first pattern jacket produced by the Richmond Bureau was made of a very fine-quality cadet grey cloth, and had a nine button front. The collar, shoulder straps and cuffs were trimmed with either tape or piping, which was often in branch colour. Belt loops were probably attached, and lining was of a coarse homespun cotton cloth inaccurately called 'osnaberg' in the South during the Civil War. The first trousers supplied were probably made from the same

until at least 1862 by uniform supplies from state government, and local volunteer aid societies. Organised in hundreds of Southern towns and hamlets, the latter raised funds, bought materials, and made frock coats, trousers, shirts, hats, overcoats, shoes, etc. for the troops in the front line.

The first Confederate Clothing Bureau was established on Pearl Street in Richmond, Virginia, by the end of August 1861. Run by Major J. W. Ferguson, it was described as follows shortly after it began manufacture: 'Every portion of the work has its appropriate department. In the upper story of the building is the cutting room, under the direction of superintendents, and lively with the noise of shears. Lower down is the trimming room. Then the department for letting out the making of the clothes, the work being given out to the wives and relatives of the soldiers, and to poor and deserving needlewomen. Lastly comes the packing department, where the clothing, blankets, &c., are packed and forwarded to the camps.' Other bureaus were eventually established

Opposite

Private J. P. Sellman, Company K, 1st Virginia Cavalry, wears another example of a Richmond Depot, second pattern uniform. USAMHI/photo by Jim Enos.

Private Bartos Jeffcoat, from Lexington, South Carolina, enlisted in the Congaree Cavaliers, a unit which became Company B, cavalry battalion of the Holcombe Legion. After reorganisation into Company D, 7th South Carolina Cavalry, he died from disease in the Federal prison camp at Elmira. He wears an example of the third pattern jacket issued by the Richmond Clothing Depot. S.C. Confederate Relic Room & Museum, courtesy of W. C. Smith.

regimental commanders requested and received uniforms for their commands which featured trim on jackets and/or trousers which were unique to their units, e.g. in 1862 Colonel W.E. Starke required a 'stripe on the pants for his Regt. [60th Regiment Virginia Volunteers] & a bar on the shoulder' of their jackets.

Whilst the dress regulations specified a 'Forage cap for officers ... similar in form to that known as the French kepi,' the pattern of 'uniform cap' to be worn by enlisted men in 1861 was not given but, according to E. Crehen's accompanying lithographs, appears also to have been based on the French chasseur pattern. This consisted of a low, countersunk crown, with a straight visor made of two pieces of leather sewn over a cardboard stiffener. A number of enlisted men's caps of probable quartermaster department manufacture survive based on this pattern. Others are of the forage cap pattern, with higher crown and flat top. Many follow 1861 regulations with grey tops and branch coloured, or black, bands, whilst others were either based on the revised 1862 pattern with branch colour tops, or were simply plain grey. Photographs often feature the black oilskin cap covers which were formally prescribed in January 1862 for wear in 'bad weather'.

A second pattern jacket was issued by the Richmond Bureau possibly as early as the Spring of 1862. Generally without trim except occasional piping on shoulder straps and/or collar, they were otherwise based on the cut of the first pattern. Surviving examples indicate that cloth being used by this time varied from a coarse wool, dyed cadet grey, called kersey, to a rough, dark greenish gray woolen material. A third type of jacket produced by the Richmond Bureau by the beginning of 1863 was the product of the Confederacy's purchasing operations abroad. Again based on the same basic shell jacket pattern, it was minus trim, shoulder straps and belt loops, and was made of heavy dark blue/grey kersey spun and woven in England, and brought through the Federal blockade. The arrival of this cloth in Richmond caused considerable interest as one Southern newspaper recorded in February 1863: 'Quite an excitement is going on at the Clothing Bureau of the Quartermaster's Department since the arrival of cloth for uniforms of English manufacture. So great is the rush of officers for suits that a guard, with fixed bayonets, is placed at the door to ensure order. Citizens on the sly are trying to rehabilitate themselves from the Government stores. Eight examples of this type of jacket survive. That worn by Corporal E. F. Barnes, 1st Company, Richmond Howitzers, was worn at the

material as the jackets, and usually had only two front pockets. Some had a watch pocket, and either a belt or holes for laces over a vent at the back to adjust for size. There were no belt loops, and many had buttons for braces. Most had a small slit at the bottom of each leg seam. Members of the South Carolinian brigade, commanded by General Joseph Brevard Kershaw, had been the beneficiary of uniforms supplied by the Richmond Depot by July 1862, as Colonel D. Wyatt Aiken, commander of the 7th South Carolina Volunteers, remarked: 'One of the Regiments of this Brigade is dressed in a remarkably neat and comfortable uniform which cost (for roundabout and pants) only eleven dollars to the man. A private could not buy the jacket for that in Richmond. The other two regiments are now being uniformed by the Government in the same way.' During these early stages of issuance some

Jacket (left) worn by Private Alfred M. Goodwin of Sturdivant's Virginia Battery. Made of dark cadet grey kersey by Peter Tait of Limerick, Ireland, the red collar and cuffs are post-war additions. Back (centre) of same. Detail (right) showing Virginia state seal buttons. Alan Thrower.

surrender of Lee's army at Appomattox Court House in 1865. Jackets of the same English cloth, but with five-button fronts and utilising shoulder straps as belt loops, are also believed to have been made at a clothing depot established at Charleston, South Carolina, by the end of 1862.

Caps issued later in the war provide further examples of economy measures made by C.S. clothing bureaus. That worn by Private Robert W. Royall, 1st Company, Richmond Howitzers, has dark blue-grey sides, red wool band and crown, and is minus a chin strap, with a visor made from layers of thin card glued together, covered with black painted cloth, and edged with leather binding.

Another pattern of uniform associated with the latter stages of the war, was also run through the boxes Tait, a clothing manufacturer of Limerick in Ireland, who earlier had clothing contracts with the British army in the Crimea, six examples of the jacket supplied with this uniform survive. Three were worn

Cap worn by Private Robert W. Royall, 1st Company, Richmond Howitzers, with dark blue-grey kersey sides, and red wool band and crown. Author's collection.

by members of the Army of Northern Virginia; one owner unknown, but found in Virginia; one from a member of the Fort Fisher garrison, and one from a person guarding Quartermaster Stores in Greensboro, North Carolina. All were made from dark cadet grey English kersey with a strong blue cast, and originally had an eight-button front, and a linen lining. That worn by Private Garrett Gouge of the 58th North Carolina has a blue piped collar and shoulder straps. The trousers supplied with the jacket worn by Sergeant M. Glennan of the 36th North Carolina were made of the same cadet grey cloth with red piped seam stripes. Combined with sky blue trousers, which were often captured from the Federal army, these mid-to late-war dark grey jackets were cause for frequent comment and incident. A Federal infantryman who talked to some pickets of a South Carolina regiment in Tennessee in late September 1863, described them as 'better dressed than we are, their uniforms being apparently new .... The Carolinians' uniform is bluish gray ... with sky blue pants.' According to D. Augustus Dickert, who served in Company H, 3rd South

Carolina Volunteers, these uniforms consisted of 'a dark-blue round jacket, closely fitting, with light-blue trousers.' Confederate soldiers wearing these uniforms often exposed themselves to the dangers of being mistaken for Federal troops. Later that year, members of the same unit wearing dark grey jackets were fired on by elements of the 7th South Carolina.

At the beginning of the war, Confederate officers were required to wear regulation frock coats with full rank insignia on collar and sleeves, which they paid for at their own expense. This resulted in their being easy targets for Federal sharpshooters. Hence, a circular from the Adjutant & Inspector General's Office, dated 3 June 1862, permitted them to purchase a quarter-master-issue fatigue uniform in the field including a plain grey jacket with rank insignia on collar only. Finally an 1864 General Order allowed them to draw enlisted clothing on the same basis as other ranks, once all the men had been supplied. On 16 November 1863, Lieutenant Elliott Welch of the Hampton Legion of South Carolina wrote to his mother: '... our clothing is still in the Qr. master's storehouse. I recently went to town to purchase a pair [of trousers] & was treated with indifference by a few upstart clerks'. This suggests that Welch, like many other officers, preferred by this time to purchase enlisted men's clothing rather than pay the inflated prices of civilian suppliers. After being on picket duty in June 1864, he wrote that he '... felt a bullet go thro' my jacket sleeve - close shave'. During this same period, he felt the need to change from blue trousers (presumably sky blue) to grey trousers. 'Having had a gun, or pistol, pointed at me on several occasions by some of our men[,] I procured a pair of nice gray pantaloons ... While out scouting[,] a pair of blue trousers with one of our dark gray jackets is apt to make a man think a Yank is in front of him.'

In the West, the Confederate Army of Tennessee received uniforms from three general bureaus, established at Columbus, Atlanta and Athens, in Georgia. The Columbus Bureau was described by the Southern press as being 'second only to the chief department at Richmond.' In January 1863, it occupied 'four, or perhaps five, large buildings, all of which are filled from cellar to garret, either by busy operatives or with army supplies. Over 15,000 suits of soldiers' clothing, manufactured in the city and surrounding country, are now stored away in one of the Government warehouses. The material of which this clothing is made was manufactured exclusively in Columbus. Over 40,000 soldiers' caps, manufactured from similar materials, now lie here awaiting requisitions from the proper army officials.' Surviving jackets

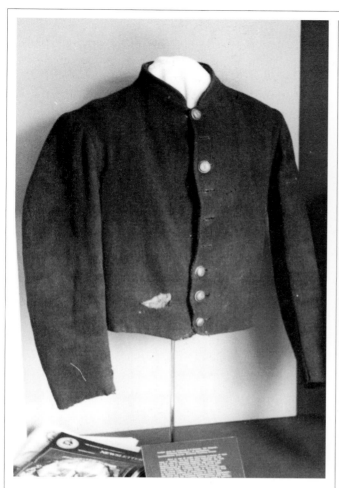

Jacket (left) worn by E. F. Barnes, 1st Company, Richmond Howitzers. Made of English cadet grey wool kersey run through the Federal blockade. Back (centre) of same. Detail (right). Alan Thrower.

issued from this source were made from grey wool jean, faded today to a butternut colour, and usually have six-button fronts. Made with a slightly longer body than the Richmond Depot pattern, they also have medium blue wool kersey or wool flannel collars and straight cuffs. A member of the 4th Florida Infantry issued with uniforms from the Columbus bureau during this period recalled: 'The coats are dark and light gray (mostly with blue collars and cuffs ... it is a worsted cross between cassimere and jeans, very warm and desireable...)' Later Columbus Depot jackets had exterior pockets sewn into the left breast.

Much of the cloth for these depots came from textile mills like the Sweetwater Factory at Marietta, the Eagle Factory in Columbus, and the Ivy Woolen Mill at Roswell, Georgia. The latter by March 1862 run by Roswell King's grandsons, Thomas Edward and James Roswell King, negotiated a contract with the Confederate Government to produce a specified quota of woollen cloth, in return for which the Confederacy agreed to furnish workmen and

Columbus Depot jacket, worn by Elijah Woodward, 9th Kentucky Infantry, ca. November 1862. Kentucky Military History Museum/courtesy of Geoff Walden.

materials. Despite wartime shortages of lubricants and spare parts for the machinery, the Kings still managed to produce about 15,000 yards of high-quality woollens every month, and thousands of Confederate volunteers consequently found themselves in receipt of jackets, caps or trousers of a dark bluish-grey cast called 'Roswell gray.'

Surviving jackets believed to have been manufactured at the Atlanta Bureau during 1864 were made from a rough handloomed wool resembling salt-and-pepper burlap which produced a greenish-grey cast. Fastened by six buttons, they were devoid of trim and minus shoulder straps and belt loops. A peculiarity of these jackets was the cut of the collar, which came to within about an inch of the edge of the coat on the right side, and was flush with the edge on the left. Thus, when fastened, the collar came together in the centre.

Clothing bureaus in Alabama were supplied with cloth from mills such as Barnett Micon & Company at Tallassee, and Phillips, Fariss & Company of Montgomery. Jackets produced at Tuscaloosa, Marion and Montgomery were made of woolen jean with dark blue collars of the same material. All surviving examples have five-button fronts, one exterior pocket which varies from one side of the jacket front to the other, and linings of cotton osnaberg. Two surviving jackets have what appear to be original wooden buttons attached, which illustrates the shortage of metal buttons in the South towards the end of the war. That worn by Silas Calmes Buck, Co. D, 12th Mississippi, had collar and cuffs of green wool twill material.

From 1861, brown cloth was supplied to the Confederate Quartermaster Department in great abundance by southern textile mills such as that owned by William Gregg at Graniteville, South Carolina. Although drained of its work force as local men volunteered for Confederate military service, the Graniteville Manufacturing Company began to supply 'BROWN GOODS' to the Richmond quartermaster authorities as early as October of that year. By March 1862, 'brown drilling at nineteen cents per yard' was supplied to Richmond on a regular basis which lasted until at least 1864. A dye made from copperas and walnut hulls, which produced a colour popularly known as 'butternut', was used extensively in the South later in the war. A jacket believed to have been

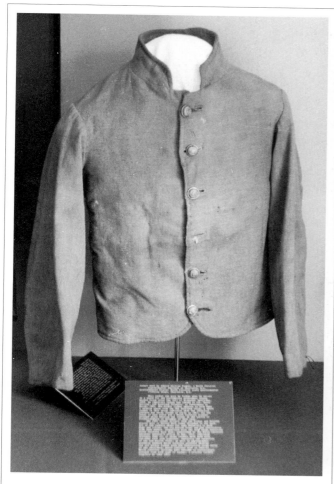

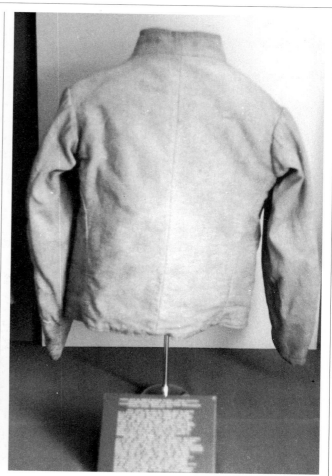

Jacket (left) worn by Edward William Tucker, a North Carolina quartermaster employee at Charlotte, North Carolina. Made of wool on unbleached cotton warp, oxidation has probably changed its colour from grey to brown. Back (centre) of same. Detail (right) showing Maryland state buttons. Alan Thrower.

worn by Charles A. Parkins, an Englishman who served in the 3rd Louisiana Infantry, provides an excellent example of later war homespun butternut. Held in the collection of the Royal Artillery Institution at Woolwich until recently, the material is a beige or light brown wool and cotton 'lindsey-woolsey' mixture, flecked with white and light blue, with a texture like hessian. The weft is apparently wool dyed butternut, or marmalade, with a warp of cotton. Based on the third pattern produced by the Richmond Bureau, it was originally fastened by six Louisiana State Seal buttons, had closed cuffs, and an exterior pocket on the left breast. Although a number of surviving garments of this colour are believed to have resulted from the oxidation or discolouration of the original grey cloth, the Parkins jacket was apparently originally brown.

The most bizarre cloth used to provide cheap uniforms in the Confederacy was a type of material called 'wool plains', which was undyed, natural

Jacket (left) of light brown wool and cotton "lindsey-woolsey" mixture worn by Charles A. Parkins, an Englishman who served in the 3rd Louisiana Infantry. Back (right) of same.

Detail (bottom left) showing flecked weave and 'Pelican' state button. Alan Thrower.

Confederate infantryman in late war Quartermaster-issue uniform, surrounded by accoutrements.

The infantryman of the Army of Northern Virginia (centre) is wearing an 'English blue', eight-button shell jacket with shoulder straps of the type made by Peter Tate, an Irish clothing manufacturer. His trousers are wool-and-cotton homespun. His high-crowned, mid-grey, enlisted man's infantry kepi is made from inexpensive cotton jean cloth and finished with a mid blue band of the type manufactured by a clothing depot in the Deep South. He is armed with a Short Enfield Rifle with sabre bayonet, and accoutred with cartridge box on belt, cap pouch, haversack and strap, canteen and strap. Note that his straps are shortened and knotted in order to prevent haversack and canteen banging against his thigh, as this was an impediment to the Civil War infantryman. Infantry 'I' buttons (top centre); tin drum canteens (top right); sabre bayonet and waist belt plates (centre right); haversacks (bottom right); cap pouches (bottom); cartridge boxes (left). Painting by Richard Hook.

coloured wool. A member of the 2nd Missouri Infantry, a regiment organised near Springfield in the Spring of 1862, recalled that 'the cloth was of rough and coarse texture, and the cutting and style would have produced a sensation in fashionable circles; the stuff was white, never having been colored, with the exception of a small quantity of dirt and a goodly supply of grease - the wool had not been purified by any application of water since it was taken from the back of the sheep.' When members of this regiment captured an enemy picket later that year, the Federals, finding themselves 'surrounded by men dressed IN WHITE ... seemed bewildered and somewhat frightened.' Similarly, during February 1863 the 3rd Louisiana Infantry, commanded by Colonel Jerome B. Gilmore, received 'a new uniform, which they were ordered to take, much against their express wishes. The material was a very coarse white jeans...' Some of the unit suggested 'the propriety of wearing the new white uniforms on the approaching [Steele's Bayou] expedition, which, it was known, would be among the swamps of the Yazoo valley in Mississippi. The suggestion was almost universally adopted, affording a rare opportunity to give the new clothes a thorough initiation into the mysteries of a soldier's life.'

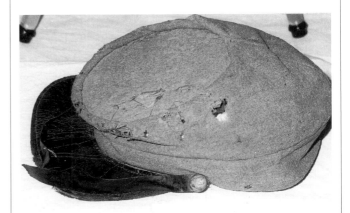

Kepi worn by R. C. Anderson, 2nd Kentucky Infantry, ca. 1863.
Kentucky Military History Museum/courtesy of Geoff Walden.

Bibliography

General works

Todd, Frederick P., *American Military Equipage 1851-1872*, 3 vols., Providence, R.I., 1974-1978.

Todd, Frederick P., *American Military Equipage 1851-1872*, Vol. II, 'State Forces', New York, 1983.

Editors of Time-Life Books, *Echoes of Glory: Arms and Equipment of the Confederacy*, Alexandria, Virginia, 1991.

The Company of Military Historians, *Military Uniforms in America - Long Endure: The Civil War Period, 1852-1867*, Novato, California, 1982.

Dyer, Frederick H., *A Compendium of the War of the Rebellion*, Des Moines, Iowa, 1903; reprinted, 3 vols., New York, 1959.

Scott, Robert N. (compiler), *The War of the Rebellion: A Compilation of the Official Records of the Union and Confederate Armies*, Washington, 1880 - 1901.

Dornbusch, Charles E., *Military Bibliography of the Civil War*, 3 vols., New York, 1961-1967.

Amann, William Frayne, *Personnel of the Civil War*, 2 vols., New York, 1961.

Tancig, W. J., *Confederate Military Land Units 1861-1865*, New York, 1967.

Crute Jr., Joseph H., *Units of the Confederate States Army*, Midlo-thian, Virginia, 1987.

Albaugh III, William, *Confederate Faces*, California, 1970.

Albaugh III, William, *More Confederate Faces*, California, 1972.

Turner, William A., *Even More Confederate Faces*, Orange, Virginia, 1983.

Serrano, D. A., *Still More Confederate Faces*, New York, 1992.

Thomas, Michael R., *A Confederate Sketchbook*, New Jersey, 1981.

Part 1: State Issue

South Carolina

Cauthen, C. E., *South Carolina Goes to War, 1860-1865*, North Carolina, 1950.

Capers, Ellison, 'South Carolina', in *Confederate Military History*, Vol. V, Atlanta, Ga., 1899.

Salley, A. S. (compiler), *South Carolina Troops in Confederate Service*, 3 vols., Columbia, S.C., 1913-1930.

McCaslin, Richard B., *Portraits of Conflict - A Photographic History of South Carolina in the Civil War*, Fayetteville, 1994.

Caldwell, J. F. J., *The History of the Brigade of South Carolinians*, Dayton, Morningside Press, 1984 (reprint).

Bigham, John Mills (comp.), 'Palmetto Soldiers - An Album of South Carolina Confederate Soldiers', *Military Images*, Vol. XI, No. 6 (May-June 1990).

Mississippi

Hooker, Col. C. E., 'Mississippi', in *Confederate Military History*, Vol. VII, Atlanta, Ga., 1899.

Rowland, Dunbar (compiler), *Military History of Mississippi 1803-1898*, Jackson, Mississippi, 1908.

Rietti, J. C. (compiler), *Military Annals Of Mississippi*, Spartanburg, S.C., 1976.

Moneyhon, Carl, & Roberts, Bobby, *Portraits of Conflict - A Photographic History of Mississippi in the Civil War*, Fayetteville, Arkansas, 1993.

Bearss, Edwin C., *Decision in Mississippi*, Jackson, Mississippi, 1962.

Adjutant General, Mississippi, *Annual Report* (for 1860), Jackson, Miss., 1861.

Orders of the Military Board of the State of Mississippi, Jackson, Miss., 1861.

Florida

Florida, Board of State Institutions, *Soldiers of Florida* in the Seminole Indian, Civil, and Spanish-American Wars, Live Oak, Fla., 1909.

Dickison, Col. J. J., 'Military History of Florida', *Confederate Military History*, Vol. XI, Atlanta, Ga., 1899.

Davis, W. W., *The Civil War and Reconstruction in Florida*, New York, 1913.

Coles, David et al, 'The Florida Issue', *Military Images*, Vol. XIV, No. 4 (January-February 1993).

Alabama

Wheeler, Lieut. Gen. Joseph, 'Alabama', *Confederate Military History*, Vol. XI, Atlanta, Ga., 1899.

Fleming, Walter L., *Civil War and Reconstruction in Alabama*, New York, 1905.

Owen, Thomas. M., 'The Military Forces of Alabama', *Alabama Historical Quarterly*, I (1939), 40-50.

Brooks, Ross, 'Confederate Uniforms, Part 1, Alabama', *Minie News*, September 1985.

Rodgers, Thomas, 'Uniforms of the Confederacy - Plate 79: 1st Volunteer Regiment, Alabama Militia, 1857-1861', *Journal, Confederate Historical Society*, Vol. XX, No. 1, (Spring 1992), 20-22.

Rodgers, Thomas and Field, Ron, 'Uniforms of the Confederacy - Plate 80: 2nd Volunteer Regiment, Alabama Militia, 1860-1861', *Journal, Confederate Historical Society*, Vol. XX, No. 2, (Summer 1992), 36-39.

Georgia

Derry, Joseph T., 'Georgia', *Confederate Military History*, Vol. VI, Atlanta, Ga., 1899.

Thomas, Thomas, W., *History of the Doles-Cook Brigade, Army of Northern Virginia*, C.S.A., Atlanta, Georgia, 1903.

Bryan, T. Conn, *Confederate Georgia*, Athens, Ga., 1953.

Jones, Charles T., *Georgia at War, 1861-1865*, Atlanta, Georgia, 1909.

Candler, Allen D. (ed.), *The Confederate Records of the State of Georgia*, 4 vols., Atlanta, Georgia, 1909-1910.

Hill, Louise B., *Joseph E. Brown and the Confederacy*, Chapel Hill, N.C., 1939.

Kerksis, Sydney C. (ed.), 'Uniform and Dress of the Army of Georgia,' *Military Collector & Historian*, XIII (1961), pp. 122-124.

Brooks, Ross, 'Confederate Uniforms, Part 4, Georgia', *Minie News*, November 1985.

Warren, Richard, 'Confederate Military Equipage: Georgia Jackets', *Journal, Confederate Historical Society*, Vol. XVII, No. 4, (Winter 1990), 94.

Lousiana

Bergeron Jr., Arthur W., *Guide to Louisiana Confederate Military Units 1861-1865*, Baton Rouge, La., 1989.

Works Project Administration, Louisiana, MS, 'Historical Militia Data on Louisiana Militia', 1851-1872 (typesrcipt at USAMHI).

Dimitry, John, 'Louisiana', *Confederate Military History*, Vol. X, Atlanta, Ga., 1899.

Bragg, Jefferson Davis, *Louisiana in the Confederacy*, Baton Rouge, La., 1941.

Moneyhon, Carl, & Roberts, Bobby, *Portraits of Conflict - A Photographic History of Louisiana in the Civil War*, Fayetteville, Arkansas, 1990.

Jones, Terry L., *Lee's Tigers: The Louisiana Infantry in the Army of Northern Virginia*, Baton Rouge, La., 1989.

Moore, Allison, *He Died Furious*, Baton Rouge, La., 1983.

Brooks, Ross, 'Confederate Uniforms, Part 6, 'Louisiana', *Minie News*, February 1986.

Texas

Roberts, Col. O. M., 'Texas', *Confederate Military History*, Vol. XI, Atlanta, Ga., 1899.

Henderson, Harry M., *Texas in the Confederacy*, San Antonio, Texas, 1955.

Oates, Stephen B., *Confederate Cavalry West of the River*, Austin, Texas, 1961.

Fitzhugh, Lester N., *Texas Batteries, Battalions, Regiments, Commanders and Field Officers, Confederate States Army, 1861-1865*, Midlothian, Texas, 1959.

Wright, Marcus (comp), and Simpson, Harold B. (ed.), *Texas in the War, 1861-1865*, Hillsboro, 1965.

Virginia

Wallace, Jr. Lee A., *A Guide to Virginia Military Organizations 1861-1865*, Lynchburg, Va., 1986 (revised edition).

Manarin, Louis H., and Wallace, Jr. Lee, *Richmond Volunteers 1861-1865*, Richmond, Va., 1969.

Manarin, Louis H. (ed.), *Richmond At War - Minutes of the City Council 1861-1865*, Chapel Hill, N.C., 1966.

Hotchkiss, Major Jed., 'Virginia', *Confederate Military History*, Vol. III, Atlanta, Ga., 1899.

Wallace, Jr., Lee A., and Finke, Detmar H., 'Virginia Military Forces, 1858-1861: The Volunteers of the Second Brigade, Fourth Division', *Military Collector & Historian*, X, 61-70; 95-101; XI, 70-79.

Arkansas

Harrell, Col. John M., 'Arkansas', *Confederate Military History*, Vol. X, Atlanta, Ga., 1899.

Fletcher, John Gould, *Arkansas*, Chapel Hill, N.C., 1947.

Woodruff, W. E., *With the Light Guns in '61-'65...*, Little Rock, Ark., 1903.

Wright, Marcus J., *Arkansas in the War, 1861-1865*, Batesville, Ark., 1963.

Moneyhon, Carl, & Roberts, Bobby, *Portraits of Conflict - A Photographic History of Arkansas in the Civil War*, Fayetteville, Arkansas, 1987.

Staff & contributors, 'Western Confederates: An Album of Rebs from the Trans-Mississippi West', *Military Images*, Vol. XVI, No. 2 (September-October 1994), pp 6-19.

Tennessee

Porter, James E., 'Tennessee', *Confederate Military History*, Vol. VIII, Atlanta, Ga., 1899.

Lindsley, John B., *The Military Annals of Tennessee, Confederate, First Series...*, Nashville, Tenn., 1886.

Wright, Marcus J., *Tennessee in the War, 1861-1865*, New York, 1908.

Civil War Centennial Commission, *Tennesseans in the Civil War*, 2 vols., Nashville, Tenn., 1964.

Temple, Oliver P., *East Tennessee and the Civil War*, Cincinnati, Ohio, 1899.

North Carolina

Clark, Walter (ed.), *Histories of the Several Regiments and Battalions from North Carolina in the Great War 1861-1865*, 5 vols., Raleigh, N.C., 1901.

Manarin, Louis H. (comp.), *North Carolina Troops 1861-1865: A Roster*, 13 vols., Raleigh, N.C., 1988 (second printing).

Mast, Greg, *State Troops and Volunteers - A Photographic Record of North Carolina's Civil War Soldiers*, Vol. 1, Raleigh, N.C., 1995.

Mast, Greg, 'Tar Heels', *Military Images*, Vol. XI, No. 2 (November-December 1989), pp 6-31.

Warren, Richard, 'Uniforms of the Confederacy - Plate 72: North Carolina State Issue Uniforms, 1861-1865', *Journal, Confederate Historical Society*, Vol. XVIII, No. 2, (Summer 1990), 45-52.

Missouri

Moore, Col. John C., 'Missouri', *Confederate Military History*, Vol. IX, Atlanta, Ga., 1899.

Bevier, R. S., *History of the First and Second Missouri Confederate Brigades, 1861-1865*, St. Louis, Mo., 1879.

Parrish, William E., *Turbulent Partnership: Missouri and the Union, 1861-1865*, Columbia, Mo., 1963.

Westover, John G., 'The Evolution of the Missouri Militia, 1804-1919', MS doctoral thesis, University of Missouri.

Staff & contributors, 'Western Confederates: An Album of Rebs from the Trans-Mississippi West', *Military Images*, Vol. XVI, No. 2 (September-October 1994), pp 6-19.

Kentucky

Johnston, Col. J. Stoddard, 'Kentucky', *Confederate Military History*, Vol. IX, Atlanta, Ga., 1899.

Thompson, Ed. Porter, *History of the First Kentucky Brigade*, Cincinnati, Ohio, 1868.

Coulter, E. Merton, *The Civil War and Reconstruction in Kentucky*, Chapel Hill, N.C., 1926.

Federal Writers Project (W.P.A.), 'Military History of Kentucky, Frankfort,' Ky., 1939.

Maryland

Johnson, Brig. Gen. Bradley T., 'Maryland', *Confederate Military History*, Vol. II, Atlanta, Ga., 1899.

Culver, Frank B., *Historical Sketch of the Militia of Maryland.*, Annapolis, Md., 1908.

David Mark, 'Maryland Troops in the Confederate Army', *Military Images*, Vol. X, No. 5 (March-April 1989), pp 4-30.

Warren, Richard, 'Confederate Military Equipage: Maryland Crosses...', *Journal, Confederate Historical Society*, Vol. XVII, No. 4, (Winter 1990), 94.

Part 2: Confederate Quartermaster Issue

Serious research into Confederate Quartermaster issue uniforms is embroyonic. The best work published to date is that of Leslie D. Jensen: 'A Survey of Confederate Central Quartermaster Issue Jackets', Parts 1 & 2, in *Military Collector & Historian*, Vol. XLI, No. 3 (Fall, 1989) & No. 4 (Winter, 1989). The Time-Life volume 'Arms and Equipment of the Confederacy' in the series *Echoes of Glory* (1991) contains photographic evidence from some of the best museum collections in the US. In 1987 the Museum of the Confederacy published a Catalogue of Uniforms which described many items of uniform in its collection, but provides photographs of only a few. Numerous references to the issuance of uniforms of quartermaster provenance may also be found in published memoirs, unpublished diaries and letters, and newspapers of the time.

Civil War Directory

This directory is a comprehensive guide for American Civil War re-enactors, historians, art collectors, modellers and wargamers.

American Re-enactment Groups

Big battle re-enactments in America can boast upwards of 6,000 troops. At the Gettysburg anniversary re-enactment in 1988 over 14,000 men took part. Many British re-enactors travel to the States during the summer to take part with members of American re-enactment groups. The following is a list of some of the hundreds of groups in the States.

5th New York Volunteer Infantry, Duryee's Zouaves. Contact: P.O. Box 1601 Alexandria VA 22313. The 5th New York is one of the oldest re-enactment units in the States and its captain is the noted American Civil War historian, Brian Pohanka. During the American Civil War, the original 5th New York boasted dozens of Englishmen in its ranks, some of them Crimean War veterans.

28th Massachusetts Volunteer Infantry. Contact: Guy Morin, PO Box 108, Auburn MA 01501. Phone: 5088323175.

48th New York Volunteer Infantry. Contact: Lou Evans, 1321 Hammerhead Lane, Virginia Beach VA 234646326.

111th Pennsylvania Volunteer Infantry Company I. Contact: Patrick A. Tarasovitch, 9800 Mark Road, Erie, PA 16509.

28th Pennsylvania Volunteer Infantry, Company C. Contact: Andy Waskie, G.A.R. Museum. 4278 Griscom Street, Philadelphia, PA 19124. Phone: 215-2896484.

56th Pennsylvania Volunteer Infantry. Contact: 1st Sergeant Grehl, RR 6 Box 6394E, Stroudsburg, PA 18360.

9th New York Heavy Artillery. Contact: Frank Cutler, 6343 Kelly Road, Sodus, NY 14551. Phone: 3154839254.

76th Pennsylvania, Keystone Zouaves. Contact: Mike Deem, 437 Corona Drive, Morgantown WV 26505.473

2nd Maine Cavalry. Contact: Major Bunker, 903 Anne Street Wharf, Baltimore MD 21231. Phone: 4102768220

81st Pennsylvania Volunteer Infantry, Company K. Contact: Theodore P. Dombroski, 768 McNair Street, Hazleton, PA 182021.

46th Illinois Volunteer Infantry. Contact: Andy Gelman, P.O. Box 1022, Highland Park, Il 60035. Phone: 708 8312648.

119th New York Volunteer Infantry Company H. Contact: Joe Billardello, P.O. Box 184, Manorville, NY 11949.

1st New Jersey Artillery Battery B. Contact: Greg Putman, 18A Anbrey Street, Summit, NJ. Phone: 201535 3745.

1st Regiment Berdan's Sharpshooters, Company B. Contact: Thomas Carton 9147829497 or John Carey 5166667348. This group is mainly based in the New York, New Jersey and Pennsylvania areas.

14th New Jersey Volunteer Infantry, Co. K. Contact: 14th NJ Volunteers P.O. Box 646 Dayton NJ 08810 or phone Steve Milek on 9085212329.

8th Michigan Volunteer Infantry, Co C. Contact: Terry McKinch, 7432 East Potter Road, Davison MI 48423.

15th New York Volunteer Cavalry, Co L. Contact: John Milteer 914 6925902.

46th Illinois Volunteer Infantry. Contact: 46th IVI P.O. Box 921, Joliet Il. 604340921.

2nd New Jersey Volunteer Cavalry, Co A. Contact; Bill Anania, P.O. Box 673, Middletown, N.J. 07748. Phone: 9086711546.

9th Pennsylvania Reserves Co A. Contact: Bob Luther, 137 Fieldgate Drive, Pittsburgh PA 15241.

1st Minnesota Volunteer Infantry Co D. Contact: James D Owens, 1639 Belvedere Boulevard, Silver Spring MD 20902.

24th Michigan Volunteer Infantry. Contact: 604 Linden Street, Big Rapids MI49307. Phone: 6167960747. 700

83rd Pennsylvania Volunteer Infantry. Contact: Robert F. Frazier, 5511 Partridge Court, Harrisburg PA 17111. Phone 717 7877111 during the day, or 7176571717 in the evenings.

Co. B Tiger Rifles, (Wheat's Tigers). Contact Peter Leccese, 9137 85th Street, Woodhaven NY 11421. Phone: 7182965897.

19th Virginia Volunteer Infantry. Contact: R. Mason, 14204 Radford Court, Woodbridge VA 22191.

1st Regiment Virginia Volunteers, Co D. Contact: Bob Lyons,15 Highfields Drive, Baltimore, MD 21228. Phone: 4107473271.

21st Mississippi Volunteers Co H. Contact: John J. Wrona,363 Quaker Highway, Uxbridge MA01569. PHone: 5082786056.

21st Virginia Volunteers Co F. Contact: Floyd Bane, 14407

Huntgate Woods Road, Midlothian VA VA 23112. Phone: 8042317852.

3rd Arkansas. Contact: Denis on 8043631903 or Terry on 7179393629.

1st Virginia Cavalry. Contact: Nick Nichols, HCR 3, Box 378A, Rochelle, VA 22736. Phone: 7039486879.

13th North Carolina Troops. Contact Rex Hovey: 9225 Surrey Road, Mint Hill NC 28227. Phone: 7045459760.

21st Regiment, North Carolina Troops. Contact: Clark Fox, 410 Keating Drive, Winston Salem NC 27104.

51st North Carolina Volunteer Infantry. Contact: Mike Murley, 910 4256836 or Mike Carraway 910 424 3963.

19th Virginia Volunteer Infantry, Co K. Contact: Ken Thaiss, 10 Carriage Way, Freehold, NJ 07728. Phone 9087804802. Fax: 9087804803.

30th Virginia Volunteer Infantry. Contact: Bruce Drummond, 6 Oakcrest Court, East Northport, NY 11731. Phone: 5167541918.

55th Virginia Volunteer Infantry. Contact: Eugene Tucceri,38 Beverley Heights, Middletown, CT 06457. Phone: 2033475750.

45th Alabama Volunteer Infantry/18th Missouri Volunteer Infantry. Contact: Mark Hubbs, 2054649751.

58th Virginia Infantry. Contact: Chris Loving, 7037240974.

1st Tennessee Volunteer Infantry, Co B. Contact: Ed Sharp, 12211 Amy Dee Lane, Medway, Ohio 45341.

7th Tennessee Volunteer Infantry. Contact: Sergeant Howard, 6096253233.

British Re-enactment Groups

In Britain, the two main umbrella organisations for American Civil War re-enactment groups are the Southern Skirmish Association, Soskan, and the American Civil War Society, the A.C.W.S. For information about joining Soskan write to, The Secretary, Southern Skirmish Association, PO Box 485, Swindon SN2 6BF. As this book went to press Soskan had the following Northern and Southern units, for prospective recruits to choose from.

2nd U.S. Artillery Battery A
2nd U.S. Sharpshooters
2nd U.S. Cavalry
18th Missouri
28th Massachusetts
42nd Pennsylvania
1st Minnesota Infantry
1st Minnesota Artillery
79th New York Veteran Reserve
6th Pennsylvania Cavalry

1st Arkansas
15th Arkansas
9th Kentucky
16th Tennessee

Private Allen H. Surrency, Company K, 61st Georgia Infantry, wears a five-button sack coat of jeans cloth. From a private collection; The Museum of the Confederacy, Richmond, Virginia.

Palmetto Sharpshooters
4th Virginia
7th Virginia Cavalry
17th Virginia
23rd Virginia
Confederate Artillery
Virginia Medical Department

For information about the A.C.W.S. write to PO Box 52, Brighouse, West Yorkshire, HD6 1JQ and you can be put in touch with one of the following Northern and Southern units

2nd U.S. Infantry
24th Michigan
2002nd Wisconsin
19th Indiana
14th Brooklyn
69th New York
2nd U.S. Artillery Battery B

The 24th Michigan can also be contacted directly by writing to Mark Gregory 82 Brierly Street, Bury, Lancashire. Phone:

01617052433.

32nd Virginia Infantry
1st Tennessee Infantry
43rd Borth Carolina Infantry
43rd North Carolina Infantry
2nd South Carolina Infantry
13th Mississippi Infantry
4th Texas Infantry
1st Louisiana Zouaves
Washington Artillery of New Orleans
Virginia Artillery

55th Virginia

Widely acclaimed as Britain's finest American Civil War re-enactment group, the 55th Virginia Infantry is an independent unit and not a member of either Soskan or the A.C.W.S. The 55th is noted for the excellence of its drill displays, authentic dress, accoutrements, and encampments. For information write to: Richard O'Sullivan, Flat 11, Grove Lodge, Crescent Grove, Clapham Common, London SW4 7AE.

Civil War Re-enactment Suppliers

The growth in living history and battle re-enactments over the past few years has led to a steady growth of specialist equipment suppliers in Britain and America who can satisfy re-enactment requirements from a forage cap to a tent peg.

Britain's largest supplier of American Civil War re-enactment equipment including haversacks, cap pouches, cartridge boxes, buttons and buckles is Alan Thrower who runs The Sutler's Store, 16 Howlett Drive, Hailsham East Sussex, BN27 1QW. Phone: 01323 840973 800.

Many British American Civil War re-enactors buy their clothing from companies in America. Some of the best Civil War uniforms renowned for their correct cut and colour are manufactured by Charlie Childs. Charlie runs his company County Cloth from 13797C, Georgetown Street NE, Paris Ohio, 44669. Phone: 2168623307

America's oldest established American Civil War re-enactment clothing supplier is the C & D Jarnagin Company P.O. Box 1860, Corinth MS 38834. Phone: 6012871977. Fax: 601 287 6033. Apart from complete uniforms Jarnagin also specialises in leather gear, footwear and tinware.

Other American firms manufacturing reproduction uniforms include Confederate Yankee P.O. Box 192, Guilford CT 06437. Phone: 2034539900. Centennial General Store, 230 Steinwehr Avenue, Gettysburg PA 17325. Phone: 7173349712.

Civil War A frame tents and shelter halves are available from Panther, 1,000 P.O. Box 32, Normantown, WV 25267. Phone 3044627718.

American Civil War Organisations

The American Civil War Round Table (UK) is Britain's leading Civil War study group and one of hundreds of American Civil War Round tables around the world. The American Civil War Round table (UK) has members all over Britain and regular meetings are held, usually in London. For further information contact, Tony Daly, 57 Bartlemas Road, Oxford OX4 1XU. Tel: 01865201216.

The Military Order of the Loyal Legion of the United States is open to direct and collateral descendants of commissioned officers of the Union Army and was founded in 1865. For information contact Robert G. Carroon, 23 Thompson Road, West Hartford, Connecticut, 01072535.

Sons Of Union Veterans of the Civil War is open to male descendants of Civil War soldiers. Write to S.U.V.C.W. 1310 Forest Park Avenue, Dept TC, Valparaiso, IN 46383.

Heritagepac is a national lobbying group dedicated to preserving American battlefields against business concerns who want to turn battlesites into shopping malls or housing developments. For information write to P.O. Box 7281, Little Rock AR 72217.

The Save Historic Antietam Foundation is aimed at preserving one of America's most important Civil War battle sites. For information contact SHAF at P.O. Box 550, Sharpsburg, MD 21782. Phone: 3014322522.

The Bucktail Regimental Association studies and celebrates the men of Pennsylvania's famous Bucktail regiments. For information contact Major Richard Miller, 1405 Blue Mountain Parkway, Harrisburg, PA 17112. Phone 7175459830.

The Fourteenth Brooklyn Regiment, New York State Militia Society of New York Inc, preserves the memory of the famous red legged devils, one of the most outstanding regiments of the Civil War. Write to Morton Berger, 2978 Ave. 'W' Apt 2A Brooklyn N.Y. 11229 for details. Mr Berger is the society's historian and curator of the 14th Brooklyn's armoury.

The Ulysses S. Grant Network promotes the study of the fabled Union general. Write for details to Donna Noralich, 238 Morse Avenue, Wyckoff N.J. 07481 USA.

The Company Of Military Historians has published many articles and plates on American Civil War regiments 1,350 and its international membership boasts the cream of Civil War scholars. For details write to The Company of Military Historians, North Main Street, CT 06498 USA.

The Sons of Confederate Veterans is open to descendants of men who fought for the South during the Civil War. For information write to Arthur Kuydenkall Jr, 193 Clover Ridge Ct, Edgewater Florida, 32141, USA.

The John Pelham Historical Association celebrates the life and times of the South's finest horse artillery commander. For membership details write to Peggy Vogtsberger, 7 Carmel Terrace, Hampton VA 23666, USA. Phone: 8048383862.

The Turner Ashby Historical Society commemorates the life and times of Southern hero, Turner Ashby. Write to Patricia

Walenista, 810 W. 30th Street, Richmond VA 23255, USA. Phone 8042323406.

The Immortal 600 Memorial Fund commemorates Confederate officers who have no marked graves. For details write to The Immortal 600 Memorial Fund, P.O. Box 652, Sparta, GA 31087.

Museums & Battlefields.

Most American battlefields have visitor centres with museums and one of the most impressive, is at the Gettysburg Military Park. Many people are put off by the drive into Gettysburg because the town itself has become a tourist trap complete with a wax museum, but the uniforms equipment and artefacts in the museum more than make up for this. The battlefield itself retains all the drama of the epic three day conflict, the largest ever fought on American soil. Walking across the scene of Pickett's charge is particularly memorable.

For brooding atmosphere though, the Antietam battlefield which has been relatively unspoiled by commercialism cannot be beaten, and it also has a fine visitors' centre, with many uniforms and artefacts on display. Twenty six miles southwest of Washington D.C. is the Manassas National Battlefield Park, encompassing both the first and Second battle. The visitor centre has good exhibits concentrating on the early period of the war, including the uniform worn by Corporal Brownell of the Fire Zouaves. The park also boasts a fine monument to Confederate general Stonewall Jackson. At Fort Sumter and Fort Moultrie in Charleston Harbour you can see where the war really began when the Confederates bombarded Sumter. Both forts have been preserved very well and both have a selection of unusual artefacts.

Of the many Western battlefields, Shiloh Miltary Park in Tennessee comes highly recommended. The battlefield itself has almost the same atmosphere as Antietam and the well laid out visitors' centre boasts a wealth of exhibits.

A number of American museums such as the West Point museum at the academy in New York State boast an impressice collection of Civil War memorabilia. The U.S. cavalry Museum at Fort Riley, Kansas, has an impressive display of Civil war memorabilia and includes an extensive collection of saddles.

Urban areas also boast impressive museums, the Smithsonian in Washington D.C. boasts a fine collection of Civil War artefacts as does Fort Ward in Alexandra, Virginia, which was the fifth largest of the 68 forts manned to protect Washington during the Civil War. The G.A.R. 2,800 Museum at 4278 Griscom Street, Philadelphia is another museum with some fine artefacts.

The Museum of the Confederacy at 1201 Clay Street Richmond VA 23219 is a must for both Yankee and Confederate military enthusiasts. The many artefacts include Jeb Stuart's plumed hat a Union Zouaves' fez picked up at First Manassas and an impressive collection of flags.

To see where the war ended, a trip to Appomattox Court House, three miles east of the town of Appomattox in Virginia is a must. It was here that Lee surrendered to Grant and an impressive

Private Edwin Sanford Gregory, Lynchburg Rifles, Co. E, 11th Virginia Infantry. Note the lighter bands of trim visible either side of his removable plastron front. Lynchburg Museum System.

reenactment of the Confederate surrender was made in the village in 1989. Today, Appomattox Court House has a brooding character all of its own.

For a flavour of American life in Britain, then a trip to the American Museum at Claverton Manor Bath is recommended. It's not specifically Civil War, but a large scale Civil War Battle is held behind the museum every year, in September.

Specialist tour operators run trips to American Civil War

battlefields and the East Coast sites conviniently grouped together in Maryland, Pennsylvania and Virginia are at most a day's drive from each other. Holts' Tours Ltd, Brtitain's oldest specialist operator runs yearly trips to a variety of battlefields. Write to Holts' Battlefields & History, Golden Key Building, 15 Market Street, Sandwich, Kent CT13 9DA for details.

Civil War Book Suppliers

More books have been written about the American Civil War than possibly World War One and Two. Not only have many modern historians written about the American Civil War, but the era spawned numerous diaries and recollections of the conflict, as well as a steady stream of regimental histories in the years following the war. The following is a list of some leading American Civil War book suppliers.

Michael Haynes, 46 Farnaby Road, Bromley, Kent BR1 4BJ (Phone: 01814601672) sells a wide variety of Civil War books, both new and secondhand. Write or call if you want to be put on his mailing list.

Kennesaw Mountain Military Antiques, 1810 Old Highway 41 Kennesaw GA 30152 USA (fax 7704240434) offer a good range of new Civil War books and reprints including such gems as *Where Bugles Called* and *Rifles Gleamed.*

Broadfoot Publishing Company 1907 Buena Vista Circle, Wilmington NC 28405 USA (phone 8005375243, fax: 9106864379) has republished both the Army Official Records and the Supplement to the Official Records, indispensable books to any American Civil War enthusiast.

Olde Soldier Books Inc, 18779 B North Frederick, Gaithersburg MD, 20879, USA (Phone: 3019632929. Fax: 301963 9556) offers a wide selection of books, autographs, letters and documents.

First Corps Books, 42 Eastgrove Court, Columbia SC292122404, USA (Phone 8037812709) has a large selection of new and difficult to obtain out of print books.

Richard A. LaPosta 154 Robindale Drive, Kensington CT 06037 USA, (Phone 2038280921) specialises in regimental histories and has many first editions.

The Command Post Dept CN P.O. Box 141, Convent Station, NJ 079610141 USA (Phone: 800 722 7344) stocks many fine books.

Longstreet House, P.O. Box 730, Hightstown, NJ 08520 USA (Phone: 6094481501) specialises in books about New Jersey, Gettysburg and New York Civil War history.

The J.W. Carson Company (CWN) 130 Myrtle Street, Le Roy, New York, 144821332 promises to supply important Cuvil War books at affordable prices, including a reprint of the 1866 edition of Campaigns of the Army of the Potomac. 3,200

The Morningside Bookshop P.O. Box 1087 Dayton, Ohio, 45401 USA with a shop at 260 Oak Street, Dayton, Ohio 45410 (Phone: 18006489710) has one of the States largest selection of Civil War books and specialises in fine reprints.

Civil War Magazines & Newspapers

One of the finest Civil War magazines on the market is Military Images which features excellent articles and original pictures of Civil War soldiers. For subscription details write to Military Images Rt 1, Box 99A, Henryville, PA 18332, USA.

North South Trader, P.O. Drawer 631, Orange VA 22960 contains many fine articles on relic collecting and uniforms.

The Civil War News, Route 1, Box 36, Tunbridge VT 05077 USA,(Phone: 8028893500. Fax: 8028895627) is a monthly 'bible' on American and international Civil War events. The Civil War News also features an extremly useful small ads section and book reviews pages.

The Union Times, U.A.D.F. Publications 5330 County Road 561, Clermont, FL 34711 USA (Phone: 9043947206) covers the Civil War Seminole War and Mexican War in South Eastern America.

The Artilleryman, Rt. 1, Box 36, Tunbridge, VT 05077 USA (Phone: 8028893500) is a specialist magazine with articles on American Civil War artillery and artillery reenactors.

America's Civil War, is a glossy magazine with plenty of intrest. Write to PO Box 383, Mount Morris Il 610547947 USA for subscription details.

In the same league is Civil War, the magazine of the Civil War Society, published by Outlook Inc, P.O. Box 770, Berryville, VA 22611, USA. Civil War Society membership details are also available from this address.

Artefacts

There are a number of good Civil War artefact suppliers, and even today some items can be picked up at reasonable prices.

The Union Drummer Boy, which has a correspondence address at 420 Flourtown Road, Lafayette Hill, PA 19444 USA and a shop at 5820 York Road, Lahaska PA 18931, offers a selection of excavated and non excavated relics. Their phone number is 6108256280.

R. Stephen Dorsey, Antique Militaria, at P.O. Box 263, Eugene OR 97440 USA (Phone: 5419373348) has a wide selection of guns and edged weapons.

The Powder Horn Gunshop Inc. P.O. Box 1001, 200 W. Washington Street, Middleburg, VA 22117, USA (Phone 5406876628) also has a wide range of items, including original belt plates.

One of the most famous centres for American Civil War artefacts is the Horse Soldier at 777 Baltimore Street, Gettysburg PA, USA (Phone: 7173340347) mailing address P.O. Box 184E, Cashtown PA 17310. A wide selection of goods are on offer and a catalogue is available at $15 for overseas customers.

Lawrence Christopher Civil War Relics, 4773 Tammy Dr. N.E., Dalton Ga 30721 USA (Phone: 8003368894 or 7062268894) has a selection of buttons, buckles, and bullets 3,600.

Civil War Videos & Art

Classic Images Productions International at PO Box 1863, Charlbury, Oxfordshire, OX7 3PD (Phone or fax: 01676635) offers theentire range of Classic Images battle reenactment videos shot at anniversary events in America and featiuring thousands of reenactors in action. They also have *Echoes of the Blue and Gray Volumes One & Two*, actual footage of Civil War veterans shot after the war with some old soldiers actually describing their experiences. *Gettysburg 75th 18631938 The last Reunion of the Blue & Gray*, also has some rare colour footage of the combatants at Gettysburg meeting for the last time. Classic Images productions has become Britain's largest emporium of videos books and art and a catalogue is available.

Civil War art has become extremly collectable during the past decade and the dean of American artists is Don Troiani, whose limited edition prints are available from Historical Art Prints, P.O. Box 660, Drawer U, Southbury, CT 064880660, USA (Phone: 2032626680). Classic Images Productions International also hope to be stocking his work.

The Heritage Studio 2852 Jefferson Davis Highway, Suite 10912. Stafford VA 22554 USA (Phone: 5406591070 or 5408996675) stocks work by the artist Donna J. Neary who has a particularly vigorous style.

Limited edition prints by Don Stivers are available from Stivers

These two men in fatigue shirts both served in the 4th Virginia Infantry. J. K. Ewing (left) enlisted in the Montgomery Fencibles, Co. G. Note his 'Sicillian'-style cap with secession cockade pinned on the side, and checkered civilian-style overshirt. His military pants have a broad dark seam stripe. Nathaniel Logan (right) joined the Liberty Hall Volunteers, Co. I, and wears the grey homespun overshirt adopted by his unit.
Herb Peck, Jr./Washington-Lee University, Lexington, Virginia.

Publishing, P.O. Box 25, Waterford VA 3,800 22190 USA.

Rick Reeves is another talented artist, whose work is available from Paramount Press Incorporated 1 West Main Street, Panama, NY 1467, USA (Phone: 7167824626)

Dale Gallon who specialises in action scenes, often opens his studio at 777 Baltimore Street, Gettysburg PA to the public. His prints are available from Dale Gallon Historical Art Inc. P.O. Box 43443, Gettysburg PA 17325 USA, (Phone: 717 334 0430).

Many businesses trade in Civil War art and one od the best known outlets for buying prints by Troiani and many other artists is Valor Art & Frame Ltd, 718 Caroline Street, Fredericksburg, VA 22401. USA. (Phone: 7033723376)

Stan Clark Military Books 915 Fairview Avenue (CWN) Gettysburg PA 17325 USA, (Phone: 7173371728, Fax: 717 3371728) also has a large selection of prints by Troiani and other wellknown artists.

Civil War Sculpture

Limited edition Civil War Sculptures have also become very collectable. The finest exponent of limited edition bronzes is Ron Tunison, who like Don Troiani is a member of the Society of American Historical Artists. Tunison began his artistic career just modelling one off clay figures, but there was so much demand for his work that he eventually turned to bronzes. 4,000 Some of his most attractive and reasonably priced work is a series of busts of Civil War personalities, including George Armstrong Custer. For details write to Historical Sculptures P.O. Box 141, Cairo, NY 12413 USA. Phone: 5186223508.

Terry Jones is another fine sculptor particularly with his recent figure of Joshua L. Chamberlain. He can be contacted at 234 Hickory Lane, Newtown Square, PA 19073 USA. Phone 6103532210.

American Civil War Model Soldiers

Paul Clarke who runs Shenandoah Miniatures at 12 Holywood Grove, Carnegie, Victoria, 3163, Australia (Fax: 0116135341443) produces a fine range of 54mm American Civil War Figures. Particularly impressive is his range of Zouaves and Paul is planning some speciality figures in the range. To go with his figures, Paul also has an extensive spare parts list.

Tradition of London Ltd, 33 Curzon Street, Mayfair London, W1Y 7AE (Phone:01714937452. Fax:01713551224) has plenty of Civil War Figures in its range. Some, including a 14th Brooklyn figure were sculpted by Andrew C.Stadden. Tradition also has some sets of toy American Civil War figures, notably a set of 114th Pennsylvania Volunteer Infantry.

Chosen Men, 74 Rotherham Road, Holbrooks, Coventry, CV6 4FE (Phone or Fax: 01203666376) produce 120mm resin figure kits of a New Hampshire Volunteer, a Tiger Zouave and a Berdan's Sharpshooter.

Fort Duquesne Military Miniatures, 105 Tristan Drive, Pittsburgh, PA, 15209 USA, (Phone 4124861823) has an extensive range of figures and busts including a kit of an 83rd Pennsylvania Volunteer and a bust of a 155th Pennsylvania Volunteer, both sculpted by Gary Dombrowksi. Fort Duquesne Miniatures are available in Britain from Historex Agents, Wellington House, 157 Snargate Street, Dover, Kent CT17 9BZ.

Terry Worster Miniatures, 8529 Ablette Road, Santee, CA, 92071, USA (Phone: 6192581888) USA has a range of exquisite portrait busts including U.S. Grant, George Meade and Thomas Meagher. He also carries a range of Civil War artillery models manufactured by Bayardi.

Michael Roberts Ltd, 2221 Hunters Road SW, Roanoke, Virginia 24015, USA (Phone: 5403427441 or 3432241) produces some fine figurekits, including a U.S. Army Brigadier General.

Miniature Militaria of Montana, P.O. Box 1166, Wolf Point, MT59201 - 116, USA, (Phone: 4066533 Fax: 406 6533510) has a fine range of 54 - 120 mm figures including Big Bethel Miniatures.

Index

Acknowledgements

The author would like to thank the following without whose assistance this book would
not have been possible: Joseph Matheson, Jr., Camden Archives; Joanna Norman,
Photographic Collection, Florida State Archives; Cory Hudgins, Curator of Photo-
graphic Collections, Museum of the Confederacy; John Bigham, Curator of Education,
South Carolina Confederate Relic Room and Museum; Elizabeth P. Bilderback,
Assistant Manuscripts Librarian, South Caroliniana Library; Norwood A. Kerr, Archival
Reference, Alabama Department of Archives and History; Gail DeLoach, Photographic
Archivist, Georgia Department of Archives and History; Pat Ricci, Confederate
Memorial Hall, New Orleans; Victor Bailey, Mississippi Department of Archives and
History; Steve Massingill, North Carolina Division of Archives and History; Dr.
Thomas Sweeney, General Sweeney's Museum of Civil War History; Claire Maxwell,
Photographs Curator, Austin History Center; Anna Peebler, Photo Archivist, Rosenberg
Library; Kathy Knox, Special Collections, Woodruff Library, Emory University; Adam
Scher, Curator of Collections, Lynchburg Museum System; Michael J. McAfee, curator
of uniforms and history, West Point Mueum; David Wynn Vaughan; Dan Snipes; Herb
Peck, Jr.; Jim Enos; Dave Mark; Russell Hicks, Jr.; Steven Lister; Alan Thrower; Robin
Forsey; Thomas Arliskas; Geoff Walden; David P. Hunter; Richard W. Hatcher, III;
Ross Brooks; Tom Rodgers; William B. Bynum; Peter Milne; Robin Smith; and Richard
Warren.